CLASSIC HILL WALKS

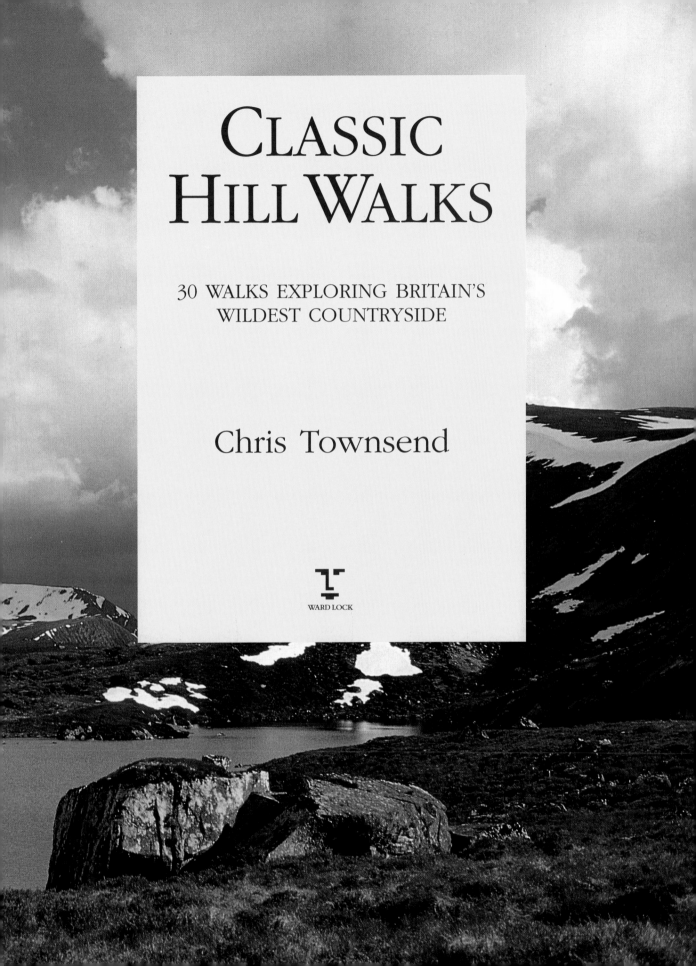

CLASSIC HILL WALKS

30 WALKS EXPLORING BRITAIN'S WILDEST COUNTRYSIDE

Chris Townsend

WARD LOCK

To Denise Thorn

A WARD LOCK BOOK

First published in the UK 1996
by Ward Lock
Wellington House, 125 Strand, London WC2R 0BB

A Cassell Imprint

Distributed in the United States
by Sterling Publishing Co., Inc.
387 Park Avenue South, New York, NY 10016–8810

A British Library Cataloguing in Publication Data block for this
book may be obtained from the British Library

ISBN 0–7063–7474–6

Typeset by Keystroke, Jacaranda Lodge, Wolverampton
Printed and bound in Slovenia by Printing House
DELO – Tiskarna by arraangement with
Korotan Ljubljana

Previous pages:
*Braeriach and
Sgor Gaoith from*

Lochan Beanaidh

Contents

INTRODUCTION

For such a small island, Britain has a surprising wealth of mountainous country. Much of the north and west is a rugged land of hills and lakes, crags and waterfalls, and while most is not true wilderness in the sense of never having been altered by human beings – only a few stony mountain tops are that – many areas are still wild and untamed with little sign of development. In the largest region – the 36,270sq km (14,000sq miles) Highlands of Scotland – you can, with careful planning, walk for days at a time without crossing a road or coming upon habitations. Further south the upland areas are smaller, but it is still possible to find solitude in places where the only sounds are those of wind and water and the cries of wild creatures.

Most walkers like a goal, and collecting summits is the obvious one in the British hills. This game can be said to have been started by Sir Hugh Munro, whose Tables listing all the Scottish peaks over 915m (3,000ft) high appeared in the second annual *Scottish Mountaineering Club Journal* in 1891. Since then, climbing all 277 of these Munros, as the separate mountains are known (there are 517 915m (3,000ft) tops), has become the aim of many walkers. Munro himself climbed all but three of them, and the first complete ascensionist was the Rev A.E. Robertson in 1901. Since then the numbers have soared, and well over 1,200 people had completed the Munros by the end of 1994. Also in Scotland are the Corbetts, 221 peaks between 762m (2,500ft) and 915m (3,000ft). This list was compiled by J. Rooke Corbett (the fourth person to complete the Munros), although it was not published during his life. Munro never explained how he decided what was a subsidiary top and what a separate mountain. With the Corbetts, however, there is a drop of at least 153m (500ft) between each summit and any adjacent higher hill.

South of the border walkers collect peaks over 610m (2,000ft) high, there being only four 915m (3,000ft) peaks in England and 15 in Wales. There are various lists in existence. A good one is that given by John and Anne Nuttall in their two-volume guide to *The Mountains of England and Wales*. They define a separate 610m (2,000ft) top as one that rises at least 15m (50ft) above its surroundings. Using this criterion, they list 181 tops in Wales and 251 in England.

It is fashionable in some circles to deplore peak bagging as mere list ticking, as treating the hills with a lack of respect. Yet, if you want to get to know these same hills, to visit all the different areas and explore the many remote corners, I can think of no better way of

Scrambling on Ill Crag en route *for Scafell Pike.*

doing so than by climbing as many different summits as possible. Peak baggers also tend to go out in any weather and all seasons, often when less motivated hillgoers prefer the comforts of home or bar. By venturing out in storms and blizzards as well as good conditions, the peak bagger experiences everything the mountain weather has to offer. Frequently it is the days of storm and snowfall that are the most memorable, as well as the most challenging. Reading the comments of those who disdain peak bagging, I also detect a whiff of moral superiority and smugness that says, 'We are superior to you, we have a greater appreciation of the hills'. This immediately makes me want to rush up as many hills as possible!

However, while overall I am in favour of peak bagging (I have to be really, being halfway through a second round of the Munros), I do think that the best way really to experience the hills is on long multi-day walks rather than by dashing up and down each one by the shortest, quickest route. Not that I am against moving fast in the hills – doing so has a magic all of its own.

There is also more to the hills than just the summits, and the walker who only aims for the heights and gives the valleys and lakes, the forests and the seashores barely a glance misses much. Indeed, it is the mix of all these features that gives the hills their unique character. Although the 30 walks described in this book concentrate on reaching summits, what they are really about is the joy of walking and living in wild, unspoilt country. Some walkers like to travel slowly, taking everything in and never hurrying. Others enjoy speed and like to cover as much distance in a day as possible. I enjoy both approaches, and the walks described here range from short strolls to arduous marathons.

While I have provided enough detail for others to follow in my footsteps, this is not primarily a guidebook – there are plenty of those already. Rather, it is an attempt to share something of what I have gained and learned from wandering in this wonderful country, something of the delight and sense of spiritual renewal that comes from spending days and nights in the hills, in the hope that this will entertain those who already undertake similar journeys and perhaps inspire those who do not to go out and experience the hills. The selection of walks is, of course, a personal one. There are likely hundreds of classic hill walks in Britain, many of them ones I have still to do. These are simply some of my favourites.

I also hope that this book will help to swell the numbers of those concerned about the preservation of the wild beauty of our hill country. The pressures for development are growing, even in those areas apparently protected with national park status, and the future for our last wild places is in the balance. New roads, conifer plantations, off-road vehicles, 'alpine' ski resorts, mining operations, tourist developments, overgrazing by deer and sheep – all these threaten the hills.

Some would say the number of walkers is detrimental too. Now, while large numbers obviously have an effect, as the eroded paths in many areas demonstrate, this damage is minimal compared with the wholesale destruction caused by industry. Most walkers stick to well-known paths. If these are kept in a state of good repair, damage through erosion can be kept to a minimum. What is needed to protect the hills, and also to enhance the experience of walkers, is to keep the hills wild and not make them easier of access by providing bridges, signposts, waymarked paths, visitor centres and more. Nor should estate or forestry roads be opened up to vehicles. The long walk-in and the need for outdoor skills in themselves keep numbers down. I believe too that the rewards for those who have learnt their hillcraft and who are prepared to put in the mental and physical effort needed to reach the heart of the wilds are far greater than the one-dimensional, picture postcard images taken away by the person who glances at the hills from a chairlift or visitor centre window, or who only experiences the hills during an unpleasant breathless stagger along a nature trail or recommended, waymarked 'safe' route. No – let us have unrestricted access to all the hills of Britain, but let us not make that access at all easy. In fact, in some areas it should be made more difficult by the removal of aids like cairns, bridges and signposts.

It is also argued by some that books like this one add to the problem by attracting new people to the hills, leading to overcrowding, erosion and loss of solitude. However, as I have said, the real threats to the hills come from commercial and industrial interests, not hillwalkers. Only public opinion and public pressure can prevent the despoliation of our remaining wild lands. If few people know about an area, who will defend it when it is under threat? If this book helps to encourage more people to walk in the hills then I will be pleased, as that is part of its purpose.

PLANNING
NOTES

SAFETY

HILLWALKING is basically a safe activity. However, there are hazards, especially for the novice. The two big risks are getting lost and getting wet and cold. Avoiding these requires good navigation skills and the correct equipment to deal with changeable weather. The latter can be bought quite easily without spending a fortune (although you can if you want to), but good gear alone does not make a person a competent hillwalker: knowing how to use it correctly is essential. Novice hillwalkers can learn from experienced companions, join a local walking club or take a course at an outdoor centre. Outdoor magazines often run skills articles and there are several books available on the subject (see Further Reading).

Snow and ice change the hills dramatically. Winter hillwalking can be more akin to mountaineering than summer walking. Learning how to use an ice axe and crampons properly is essential and I would recommend taking a course, as these are not skills you can easily teach yourself.

MAPS

The Ordnance Survey 1:50,000 Landranger maps are the standard for hillwalking and cover the whole of the British Isles. Better for detail are the 1:25,000 Outdoor Leisure series, which cover many of the popular mountain groups.

An alternative to the OS maps are Harveys 1:40,000 Walker's maps and 1:25,000 Superwalker maps. These are designed specifically for outdoor use and contain much useful information and great detail. They are also printed on waterproof material.

WEATHER

The most constant factor in Britain's weather is its change-ability. Much of the weather begins out in the Atlantic Ocean, where the meeting of air from the arctic with air from the tropics creates areas of low pressure known as depressions which sweep in, often in rapid succession, to give wet and windy weather. Because these lows come from the west it is that side of the country that has the highest rainfall, with the mountains there receiving nearly twice the annual average of eastern ones. (When I started walking in the Highlands I was told, 'If it's raining in Torridon go to the Cairngorms'. I took this advice once. It was raining in the Cairngorms too.)

Height also makes a difference to rainfall. The summit of Ben Nevis has more than twice the annual average rainfall of Fort William at its foot, while in the Lake District the Langdale Pikes have around 430cm (170in) of rain a year but Windermere, just 20km (12 miles) away only 150cm (60in). As you climb, it not only gets wetter but also colder and windier. Temperatures drop roughly 2°C (4°F) for every 305m (1,000ft) rise in altitude, while winds on the summits can be well over twice their speed in the valley below. In inversion conditions this temperature variation is reversed, with the cloud-filled valleys cold and wet but the summits sunny and warm.

Snowfall can occur in any month on the summits, especially in the Highlands, but it is usually only a serious problem from October to April, and on southern hills and in mild winters there may be little or no snow at all. Because the heaviest snow arrives on easterly airstreams, the easternmost mountains, especially the Cairngorms, receive the most cover in many years. Conditions can vary widely from year to year and from month to month, however. In some years there may be no appreciable snowfall until March, in others, there may be snow almost down to sea level at Christmas. I have walked on snow-free hills in January, only to ski on them in May.

Sunny days and even weeks occur in both summer and winter, of course. Overall, there is not much difference between the west and east in terms of temperature or hours of sunshine. There is between north and south, however, with the Highlands distinctly cooler than Dartmoor or the Brecon Beacons.

On average, the best time of year for sunny weather is spring, from mid-March to mid-June. Second best is early autumn: high pressure in September and October can bring superb weather, with frosts at night and brilliant clear days. July and August, although the warmest months, are often wet and hazy (and overcrowded and midge-ridden). Gale-force winds can occur at any time but are most likely during the winter, with early December to late February usually seeing the worst storms, and with the highest wind speeds normally occurring in the Cairngorms.

Up-to-date weather forecasts are vital for planning. Radio and television forecasts are more useful, because more up-to-date, than newspaper ones, while recorded telephone weather lines for specific mountain regions, although expensive, are the most useful of all. Where these are not available, national park visitor centres or tourist information offices can probably give a forecast.

RECORDED WEATHER FORECASTS

Weathercall: 0891 500404 (covers Dartmoor but not specifically for the hills)

Weathercall: 0891 500414 (covers the Brecon Beacons but not specifically for the hills)

Weathercall: 0891 500417 (covers the Yorkshire Dales and the Peak District but not specifically for the hills)

Lake District: 017687 75757

Mountaincall Snowdonia: 0891 500449

Mountaincall West (West Highlands): 0891 500441 and 0891 505329

Mountaincall East (East Highlands): 0891 500442 and 0891 505328

East Highlands Climbline: 0891 654668

West Highlands Climbline: 0891 654669

EQUIPMENT

Seasoned walkers will have their own views as to the best equipment. The following notes are intended to point the less experienced in the right direction, or at least towards what the author has found works for him.

FOOTWEAR

My preference is for lightweight, flexible footwear which I find more comfortable and less tiring to wear than heavier, stiffer designs. In summer I usually wear trail shoes or fell-running shoes or even, when it is really warm, sports sandals rather than boots. The idea that boots are needed for ankle support is false, most lightweight boots give minimal support in this area. However, when there is snow and ice on the hills boots are needed that can be fitted with flexible crampons. The year-round walker who only has one pair of boots should make sure that they are suitable for crampons.

There are many suitable brands and the fit is more important than the model. It is worth spending some time trying on different styles until you find the ones that fit your feet best.

Socks are important too, although how many pairs you wear is a matter of personal choice. Buy good-quality ones and wash them frequently, inside out and with a fabric softener. Once socks start to wear thin, replace them. Darning only produces rough areas that can rub and cause blisters.

CLOTHING

The most important function of your clothing is to keep out wind and rain. Waterproof outer garments are the key to this. 'Breathable' ones, that allow body moisture through, are more comfortable to wear than non-breathable, although they are not totally condensation free. It is not necessary to buy the most expensive to get the best performance. The life of a waterproof can be extended if a lightweight windproof smock or jacket is worn when it is cold and breezy but not raining. Waterproof overtrousers are useful in prolonged rain. Zipped legs allow them to be put on over boots.

As hillwalking involves high energy output, clothing that can remove the resultant sweat and body moisture quickly is best for wearing next to the skin. I have found synthetic 'wicking' fabrics such as polypropylene or poly-ester best for this base layer; traditionalists may prefer silk or wool. The material to avoid is cotton, which is cold and clammy when wet and takes a very long time to dry. I wear a lightweight synthetic top all year round, finding it cooler in summer than cotton. Quick-drying warm-wear is a good idea too, and the material I have found best here is pile or fleece. A lightweight fleece top worn over a base layer garment and under a waterproof shell will keep you warm and dry in all but the worst winter weather. Then I usually wear a heavyweight base layer plus the fleece top. In freezing conditions a lightweight down-filled top is useful as warmwear for rest stops or when camping, and takes up little room in the pack.

For legwear I prefer shorts in summer, although midges and wind often preclude the wearing of them. Otherwise, lightweight polycotton or microfibre trousers or breeches work well. These can be used in winter over long johns, although I generally wear thick synthetic trousers or salopettes then.

To ensure comfort and safety, the extremities should not be neglected. A warm hat is useful all year round and essential in winter, when I carry two, just in case I lose one. Gloves or mitts are not necessary in high summer, but most of the year I carry two pairs; a thin inner glove and a fleece-lined windproof outer mitt.

Gaiters are useful for keeping water, mud and snow out of your boots. However, I find wearing them restrictive and uncomfortable so I only do so in deep snow.

CAMPING EQUIPMENT

Tents for camping high in the hills need first and foremost to be capable of resisting strong winds. Tunnel and dome designs are now just about standard. As tents have to be carried, the weight is important too. Solo models need weigh no more than 1.5–2kg (3½–4½lb) and two-person ones 2.5–4kg (5½–8¾lb). Insect netting doors are just about essential if you are to stay sane on hot summer nights when midges are on the wing. Large vestibules in which you can store wet gear and cook in bad weather are necessary too.

Synthetic-fill sleeping bags are popular because of their resistance to damp and relatively low cost. However, even the best ones are far bulkier and heavier than down-filled bags for the same warmth, so for the backpacker down is the best choice. For three-season use, one with 500–700gms (18–25oz) of down fill with a total weight of no more than 1.5kg (3½lb) should suffice. For occasional winter use, clothing can be worn in the bag.

Some form of sleeping mat is essential in winter and all but the hardiest will use one year round. Closed-cell foam pads are lightweight and inexpensive but quite bulky. Self-inflating mats are heavier (the lightest is the excellent Therm-A-Rest Ultralight at 440gm/14oz), but can be folded up and carried inside the pack.

COOKING GEAR

The simplest and lightest stoves are those that run off gas cartridges. Butane/propane canisters can be used year round, although they are sluggish in cold weather. Alternatives are meths, petrol and paraffin. Stoves that run on the first come complete with pans and windshields and will work outside in the strongest winds. They are also very safe as the fuel is not pressurized. However, meths is not as hot as other fuels, so more has to be carried. Petrol and paraffin are the hottest-burning fuels, but the stoves are somewhat complicated to use compared with meths or gas and there is a risk, especially with petrol, of flare-ups during lighting.

Kitchen utensils need not add up to much in the way of weight, although many people carry more than is necessary. My solo kit consists of a 1 litre (1¾ pint) stainless steel pan, ½ litre (1 pint) stainless steel mug which doubles as a second pan, soup spoon, teaspoon, Swiss Army Knife, 1 litre (1¾ pint) plastic water bottle and 4 litre (7 pint) water bag. When I have a companion I take a stainless steel cookset with 1½ and 2 litre (3 and 3½ pint) pans, a plastic bowl and a 9 litre (2 gallon) water bag.

ODDS AND ENDS

Various other items help to make life in the hills safer and more comfortable. Map and compass are obviously indispensable. Also essential year round are a torch, preferably a headlamp (with spare batteries), a bivvy bag and a first aid kit, while insect repellent, sunglasses and sunscreen will all be needed at times – the last two as often in winter as in summer, in my experience. A water bottle, or thermos flask in cold weather, should be carried, along with some food.

When there is snow and ice on the hills, an ice axe and crampons will be needed. Simple lightweight ones designed for walkers are perfectly adequate. Their use should be practised on safe slopes before you venture on to potentially hazardous terrain, and you should have them ready for use – an ice axe strapped to the back of your pack might as well be at home.

Helvellyn and Swirral Edge from Catstycam.

Walking sticks – or trekking poles, to give the current trendy name – are very useful for stability when fording rivers and descending steep slopes. They also take some of the strain off your knees and back and help minimize the chance of injury. I rarely go out without mine. Collapsible ones can be strapped to your rucksack when not required.

RUCKSACKS

How big a rucksack you need depends on your ambitions. For the summer day walker, one of around 25 litres (1525 cubic in) should be big enough. Winter walkers will need a little more space, say 30–40 litres (1831–2440 cubic in), and should also look for ice axe and crampon straps on the outside. How many pockets and compartments the rucksack has and whether it closes with buckles or zips is a personal choice. Some people like lots of separate sections for organizing their gear, others a simple single compartment into which everything can be shoved.

If you intend camping out a larger rucksack will be required, and care is needed to ensure that it fits you properly. For summer weekends a 50–60 litre (3050–3660 cubic in) sack will probably be enough; for longer trips where more food has to be carried, and for winter expeditions with bulky cold-weather sleeping bags and clothing, one of 75 litres (4577 cubic in) or more may be needed.

Whatever rucksack you use it will not be fully waterproof, so liners or covers will be needed to keep your gear dry.

BOTHIES

Disused shepherds' huts, long-abandoned crofts, decaying shooting lodges and empty keepers' cottages can be found throughout the British hills, especially in the Highlands. Many are no more than four ragged walls behind which you can cower out of the biting wind. Some, however, have been restored and turned into weathertight unlocked shelters for use by hillgoers. The voluntary body that does this is the Mountain Bothies Association, to which all walkers who use bothies should belong. As well as the MBA bothies (which they do not own, but renovate with the owners' permission), there are others maintained by local estates that may be unlocked.

Bothies can be a haven in bad weather, especially in winter. They are also good refuges in summer when the midges are biting, as well as a roomy alternative to the confines of a tent. However, some bothies have become so popular that there are problems with overuse and misuse. Since 1980 two purpose-built ones in the Cairngorms have been pulled down due to problems with litter and the erosion of the surrounding areas. All bothy users should follow the MBA's bothy code:

THE BOTHY CODE

RESPECT OTHER USERS

• Don't crowd bothies out; be prepared to camp, especially when in a group or using small or popular bothies.
• Leave the bothy clean and tidy, with dry kindling for the next visitors.

RESPECT THE BOTHY

• Guard against fire risk and don't cause vandalism or graffiti.
• Take out all rubbish which you don't burn; don't leave perishable food.

RESPECT THE SURROUNDINGS

• Keep the surrounding area clean; don't use it as a toilet.
• Conserve fuel; never cut live wood.

TRANSPORT

Most walkers use cars for travelling to and from hill areas. However, many excellent walks are linear ones, leaving car-borne walkers with the problem of how to get back to their vehicle. One way for a group is to use two vehicles, and either leave one at the finish of the walk and then all travel to the start in the other, or divide into two parties, each with keys for each car. I have seen it suggested that the groups could swap car keys when they meet en route. However, the possibility of the parties missing each other in bad weather has always put me off this approach. In some areas, public transport can be used to return to the start. Minibus services in many national parks are specifically designed to convey walkers to and from popular routes.

Public transport can also be used to travel to the mountains. Cars are becoming a problem in many popular areas, especially in the summer, with car parks full and minor roads blocked – just visit Langdale in the Lake District on a sunny summer weekend to see what I mean. Public transport overcomes this and also cuts down on the pollution caused by the internal combustion engine.

I travel by public transport as often as possible. In the course of writing this book, I travelled by train and bus all the way from my home in Strathspey in Northern Scotland to Dartmoor and the Brecon Beacons to research walks. This proved much quicker (the train from Aviemore to Exeter takes 11 hours, driving would take me two days) and far more relaxing than driving.

Many people do not use public transport because of the difficulty in obtaining details of times. Two publications can help here. First is the *Great Britain Bus Timetable*, published three times a year, and obtainable from Southern Vectis, Nelson Road, Newport, Isle of Wight, PO30 1RD. Tel: 01983 522456. This book contains bus/rail interchange details. Second is the twice-yearly *Great Britain Passenger Railway Timetable*, which still covers all services and hopefully will go on doing so despite the iniquitous rail privatization plan. It is available from most large stations.

THE WALKS

DIFFICULTY

THE difficulty of a walk depends on a number of factors. Distance, navigation and terrain all play a part, while the weather is of crucial importance. A walk over rolling moorland that is easy on a clear day could be a major challenge in thick mist, while snow and ice can turn a simple ridge walk into a serious mountaineering route. A single grade for a walk is hardly adequate, so I have given gradings for navigation, terrain and winter conditions.

NAVIGATION

- **Easy** – the whole route is on clear paths.

- **Moderate** – most of the route is on clear paths, but there are sections that could be confusing.

- **Difficult** – most of the route is on rough or faint paths or across country.

- **Very difficult** – a cross-country route in featureless terrain or on steep, rocky ridges.

TERRAIN

- **Easy** – good paths, with few if any boggy or very steep sections.

- **Moderate** – some steep and/or boggy sections.

- **Difficult** – much cross-country walking, with many steep slopes and/or boggy sections and easy scrambling.

- **Very difficult** – involves sustained scrambling on steep rocks; carrying a rope is recommended.

WINTER

- **Easy** – no steep slopes.

- **Moderate** – some steep slopes that could be difficult if icy.

- **Difficult** – potentially dangerous slopes.

- **Very difficult** – a mountaineering route rather than a walk; a rope is essential.

TIME

People walk at different speeds. Some like to stride out and walk for hours without a break; others stop frequently to look at the view, study flowers, take photographs or simply have a rest. Many books give times for walks, usually based on Naismith's Rule – an hour for every 5km (3 miles) plus half an hour for every 305m (1,000ft) of ascent. This is a useful basis for estimating times, but does not allow for stops or difficult terrain. Rather than times, I have given distances. That way you can work out the rough time for the speed at which you prefer to walk, rather than wondering why I am so slow or cursing me for being too fast.

ONE

SOUTH-WEST ENGLAND

Most of England south of a line from the Bristol Channel to the Wash is a flat land with only a few low, gentle hills. Nevertheless, there is some fine walking country here – along the coasts, through the forests, over the rolling downs and beside the slow, meandering rivers. It is not hillwalking, though, and has none of that feeling of wild grandeur and freedom found in the high country. In the far south-west the land does rise up however, in the form of high heather-covered moorlands. Bodmin Moor, Exmoor and Dartmoor are all interesting walking country, but only the last compares with the hills to the north.

Dartmoor consists of two large plateaux, the North and South Moors, much of which lie above the 450m (1,500ft) contour. The first is the highest – two of the summits reaching over 610m (2,000ft) – and in some ways the wildest, although the feeling of remoteness is severely intruded upon by the presence of military firing ranges with their attendant roads and ugly buildings, a disgrace that makes a mockery of Dartmoor's national park status. The South Moor is lower and less rocky, but also less frequented and without firing ranges. On either moor you can be over 5km (3 miles) from a public road, something impossible anywhere else south of Scotland. The combined size of the two moors is 945sq km (365sq miles), a big area to explore.

A DARTMOOR CROSSING

*A most exciting, interesting and intriguing corner
of our varied world.*

John Earle, *Walking on Dartmoor*

Start/finish:	Okehampton to Ivybridge
Summits:	Belstone Tor 479m (1,571ft), Hound Tor 495m (1,623ft), Watern Tor 526m (1,725ft), Quintin's Man 552m (1,810ft), Winney's Down 539m (1,767ft)
Distance:	43km (27miles)
Navigation:	Very difficult
Terrain:	Moderate
Winter:	Easy
Map:	OS 1:25,000 Outdoor Leisure 28: Dartmoor

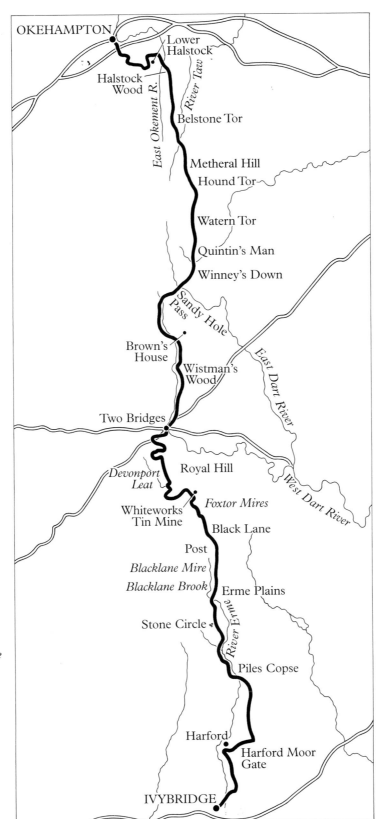

OKEHAMPTON

Lower Halstock

Halstock Wood

East Okement R.

River Taw

Belstone Tor

Metheral Hill

Hound Tor

Watern Tor

Quintin's Man

Winney's Down

Sandy Hole Pass

Brown's House

Wistman's Wood

East Dart River

Two Bridges

Royal Hill

Devonport Leat

West Dart River

Foxtor Mires

Whiteworks Tin Mine

Black Lane

Post

Blacklane Mire

Blacklane Brook

Erme Plains

Stone Circle

River Erme

Piles Copse

Harford

Harford Moor Gate

IVYBRIDGE

Left: *ponies on Belstone Tor on the northern edge of Dartmoor.*

Previous pages: *the Blackstone River on the northern edge of the South Moor, Dartmoor.*

25

With no really distinct summits and vast areas of relatively level moor, Dartmoor is an ideal place for long-distance walks. Several named ones exist, including the Two Moors Way which goes on to Exmoor, the Abbot's Way from Buckfast Abbey to Princetown, the Lich Way from Bellever to Lydford and the Mariner's Way from Ivybridge to Chagford. However, although these and other paths are marked on the maps they are often hard to follow on the ground. It is easy, though, to work out your own routes. You can go just about anywhere on the open moor, the only restriction being in the military ranges, which are out of bounds when firing is in progress. There is little firing over the summer (none at all on any of the three ranges in August), at weekends or on public holidays at the time of writing. It is always best to check, however. Otherwise plan a walk that does not cross the ranges, as I have done here. By doing this you also avoid the military tracks and the squat observation posts that, to my mind, ruin the walking inside the ranges.

The underlying rock on Dartmoor is granite. This can be seen on many of the hills in the form of clusters of large boulders known as tors. Most of the moor is covered with peat, making up a vast sponge that after heavy or prolonged rain can be very boggy to walk over. Swift streams carry this water off the moor. These can rise rapidly and be difficult to ford after storms. Heather, purple moor grass, bilberry and various grasses cover the peat, making for a rough, tussocky surface that is quite hard to walk on. The really boggy areas, known as mires, can often be identified in spring and summer by the white feathery flowers of cotton grass. If you want to keep your feet dry, stay out of these. Trees are rare, most of the high-level forests having been felled

long ago, but there are a few areas of fascinating ancient oakwoods, while in places the straight lines of modern conifer plantations encroach on the moor.

Living in northern Scotland, I do not often visit the south-west, so when I travelled down to walk on Dartmoor I wanted to see as much as possible. A walk across the moor seemed the best way to do this, so I worked out a rough route from Okehampton in the north to Ivybridge in the south. Both these towns have good public transport links, with regular buses from Exeter to Okehampton and a railway station at Ivybridge. The latter, by the way, is only marked on the most recent maps as it was opened just a few years ago.

From Okehampton I headed south-east across the edge of the moor on farm tracks to pleasant Halstock Wood and the East Okement River. Across the river the open moor begins, and there is an easy climb to the rocky summit of Belstone Tor. Here a small herd of ponies, common on Dartmoor where they have been grazed for centuries, were sheltering from the cold north wind below the small crags. To the north rich Devon farmland filled the scene, but the exciting views were to the south and west where wave after wave of empty moorland faded into the horizon. Here I had my first hint of the vastness of Dartmoor. The highest tops on Dartmoor, 619m (2,031ft) Yes Tor and 621m (2,037ft) High Willhays, can be seen to the west. Sadly, they lie in the middle of a firing range and have been desecrated with roads and buildings. Tall steel masts on which red flags are flown when firing is taking place sully many of the hilltops in and along the edge of the ranges.

Continuing south, I descended into the wide and boggy valley of the River Taw, getting my feet wet for the first of

*Belstone Tor on the
northern edge of
Dartmoor.*

many times, then climbed up over Metherall Hill to Hound Tor, said, in one of the many legends about places on Dartmoor, to be haunted by the devil who hunts here with black hounds with eyes of fire. The walk now began to take on a timeless, seamless quality as I strode on south over Watern Tor to the newtake wall (a newtake being an area reclaimed from the moor) above the dark wedge of coniferous Fernworthy Forest, then to Quintin's Man and Winney's Down, across the East Dart River above Sandy Hole Pass and on to the West Dart River. The moors flowed past with few distinctive features. Each minor swelling looked much like the last, each boggy dip was as wet as the last. The joy of walking here was in the overall feel of space and remoteness, in being surrounded by vast, untamed country. The cries of buzzards and curlews added to the sense of wildness.

At one point I caught a movement ahead. A fox was moving slowly across a patch of rough hillside a few hundred metres away. Suddenly it vanished. I waited, motionless, for a short while and then went across to investigate. As I expected, I found a large earth with several entrances dug into the moor. Thick vegetation covered the sandy ground in places, and as I stopped to see if the fox would reappear a small fox cub popped out of the long grass just a couple of metres from me. For a few seconds we stared at each other. The cub looked curious and intelligent but unafraid. Then, as quickly as it had appeared, it dropped back into the earth.

The West Dart River runs south off the North Moor down a pleasant rocky valley, boggy at its head. The best path appears to be on the true right bank, as I realized as I was trying to pick a dry route through Brown's House Bog below the ruins of Brown's House, an old farm. Just as I gave up and accepted sodden feet again, three walkers came up the valley on the far side of the river, striding over the dry ground. I tried, probably unsuccessfully, to look as though I were standing ankle deep in mud in the middle of the marsh intentionally. As with many of the streams on Dartmoor there are signs of tin mining, including the remains of a tinner's hut, along the banks. This was an important industry on Dartmoor from the twelfth to the nineteenth century and relics abound all over the moor.

Further down the West Dart is one of the three remnants of high-level primeval oak forest left on Dartmoor, Wistman's Wood. Like the other ancient woodlands, Wistman's Wood grows on a west-facing slope covered with clitter, that is rocks and boulders eroded by ice and water from the tor above. The stunted, twisted trees are no more than 5m (15ft) in height. Mossy epiphytes hang in long festoons from the branches and the trunks are covered in moss, as are the boulders that litter the ground beneath the trees. The undergrowth is thick and lush with many ferns. Inside the wood there are huge boulders with small caves between them. The whole atmosphere is one of great age, and the wood feels peaceful and calm but also mysterious and other worldly. It is easy here to believe Dartmoor's many legends of supernatural events.

South of Wistman's Wood a good path leads down to the tiny hamlet of Two Bridges, where the Cowsic River converges with the West Dart and the two roads that run east-west across the moor meet. It is near enough the centre of Dartmoor. A large hotel here provides refreshment before the South Moor is tackled.

Although lower, the walking on the South Moor is no easier than on the

North. There are even fewer tops of any note and the feeling of remoteness is just as strong. From Two Bridges I followed farm tracks and minor roads across the west slopes of Royal Hill to the disued Whiteworks Tin Mine. Just before the mine the road passes the Devonport Leat, an amazing piece of engineering built in 1790 to take water from the Cowsic River down to Devonport on the coast.

Next I crossed the large wet expanse of Foxtor Mires (wet feet again!). I read later that this bog can be dangerous, so I would advise others to stick to the edge. It was apparently the model for Great Grimpen Mire in Sir Arthur Conan Doyle's famous Sherlock Holmes story, *The Hound of the Baskervilles*. The legends of giant hellhounds such as that of Hound Tor obviously inspired Conan Doyle too.

Beyond the bog I climbed up to the open moor and headed south for Blacklane Brook past a large wooden post that marks the high point of the Blacklane, one of the old passes through the peat used by cattle drovers and tin miners, which runs between Crane Hill and Naker's Hill. Blacklane Mire further down the stream is another very moist area that ensured my feet stayed wet. As I was crossing this bog I came upon the bloated body of a drowned cow, an unpleasant sight that reminded me both of the dangers of the mires and not to drink water running through or out of these swamps.

Blacklane Brook runs into the upper Erme River, which I followed southwards. This fascinating valley holds many relics of tin mining. There were human beings on the moor long before the tinners though, and above the area known as Erme Plains I walked along a bronze-age line of standing stones to a fine stone circle called the Dancers or Kiss-In-A-Ring. In total the stone row runs for 4km (2½ miles), making it the longest in Britain – probably the longest anywhere in fact. Further down the Erme is Piles Copse, another remnant of ancient oak woodland.

Below Piles Copse the land beside the river is enclosed so I climbed east to the open moor, which I eventually left at Harford Moor Gate to descend to the church at Harford and a narrow road that led between high hedges for the last 3km (1¾ miles) to Ivybridge. If I had not been caught out by the dark (the whole crossing took me 12 hours) I would have stayed out on the open moor and descended by the Two Moors Way. As it was, I felt content if tired after crossing the hearts of both the North and South Moors in one walk.

TWO

THE
WELSH HILLS

WALES is a land of mountains, with 181 summits over 610m (2,000ft) high. You can walk from coast to coast, south to north, and be in hill country the whole way. Indeed, there is an unofficial long distance path, the Cambrian Way, that does just that, though there is no need for it – you can easily plan your own route.

The mountains can be roughly divided into three very different groups. In the south lie the Brecon Beacons and the Black Mountains, steep-sided, flat-topped mountains reaching 886m (2,900ft) in height. You can walk for miles here without dropping below 610m (2,000ft). The main features of these sandstone hills are the huge, steep north-facing slopes that rise above deep, glacier-carved hollows, or 'cwms'.

North of the Beacons the hills are lower. Just eleven tops rise above 610m (2,000ft) in Central Wales, with Pumlumon the highest. They are less immediately impressive too, having more in common with the great moorlands of the Northern Pennines than the mountains to the north or south. However, there is a sense of solitude and wildness here not found in other areas, for the hills are relatively little visited. I have not included any routes in this area here – go and discover them for yourselves!

In North Wales lies Snowdonia, a magnificent range of mountains with the roughest, steepest terrain south of the Scottish Highlands. This is wonderful walking country, especially for those who like narrow ridges and easy rock scrambles.

THE HIGH TOPS OF
THE BRECON BEACONS

*The range is an extraordinary one. I can think of no
comparison.*

Hamish Brown, *Hamish's Groats End Walk*

Start/finish:	Brecon or Cwm Gwdi
Summits:	Pen y Fan 886m (2,907ft), Cribyn 795m (2,608ft), Corn Du 873m (2,864ft)
Distance:	10km (6 miles) from Cwm Gwdi, 18km (11 miles) from Brecon
Navigation:	Moderate
Terrain:	Moderate
Winter:	Difficult
Map:	OS 1:25,000 Outdoor Leisure 11: Brecon Beacons National Park – central area

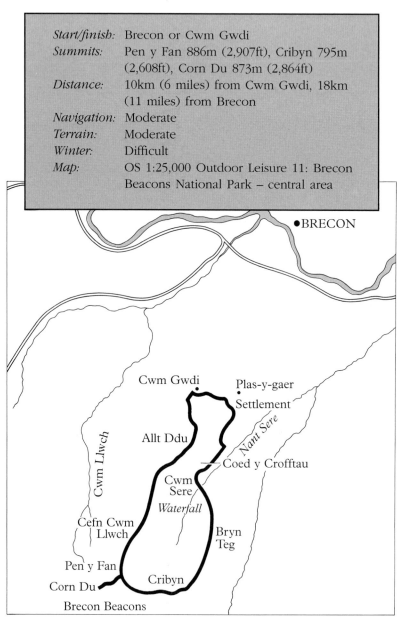

●BRECON

Cwm Gwdi

Plas-y-gaer
●
Settlement

Nant Sere

Allt Ddu

Cwm Llwch

Coed y Crofftau

Cwm
Sere

Waterfall

Cefn Cwm
Llwch

Bryn
Teg

Pen y Fan

Corn Du ●

Cribyn

Brecon Beacons

Left: *Cascades on the Naut Sere in Cwm Sere with cloud-capped Cribyn in the background, Brecon Beacons.*

South of Snowdonia, only one mountain range approaches 915m (3,000ft) in Britain: the Brecon Beacons. Lying south of the Vale of Esk, these hills are part of the 1,344sq km (519sq miles) Brecon Beacons national park. At the east end of the park are the Black Mountains; at the west, confusingly, the Black Mountain. However, it is in the heart of the park that the Beacons proper – the highest peaks – lie, just to the south of the town of Brecon. As well as being in the national park, these peaks are owned by the National Trust.

The Beacons are made of a sedimentary rock, old red sandstone, as is well shown by the distinctive horizontal strata of the northern slopes. Ripple marks from the rivers that deposited the sandstone have been found high on the summits. After the sandstone was laid down it was covered by other rocks and these softer rocks were then slowly eroded away to reveal the sandstone, although while it lay buried earth movements folded the layers and they emerged slightly tilted, dipping gently to the south-west with steep slopes to the north. These scarp slopes were steepened by erosion

during the ice age when the great cwms below the peaks were carved out.

There are various routes to the Beacons' crest, the most popular, because shortest, being that from the Storey Arms to the west. However, this route is boring and badly eroded, and is not to be recommended. The Beacons are most impressive from the north and the best ascents are from that direction.

From the Vale of Usk the Beacons make for an impressive scalloped skyline, with the summits rising above steep-backed, deep cwms split by long thin ridges. To reach the foot of the hills from Brecon you must plunge into a maze of lanes walled by high hedgerows, that climb gently through small fields and woods. In spring and summer this is a pleasant walk in itself, the banks and hedges rich with flowers. However, although this preliminary stroll takes less than an hour, those with a car will probably drive these first few kilometres.

Cwm Gwdi makes a good starting point for a round of Cribyn and Pen y Fan by way of the fine ridges of Bryn Teg and Cefn Cwm Llwch. Older maps show military ranges here, but these are

Previous pages: *Cribyn and Pen y Fan from Allt Ddu, Brecon Beacons.*

Cloud-capped Cribyn rising above the trees of Coed y Crofftau in Cwm Sere, Brecon Beacons.

not used any more and there are no access restrictions. From the road end a path leads off east below the steep slopes of Allt Ddu and past a large mound with trees on its top that is the site of the Plas-y-gaer iron-age settlement. Staying above the intake wall, the route now turns south into Cwm Sere, at the head of which can be seen the steep faces of Cribyn and Pen y Fan. Once past the attractive deciduous woods of Coed y Crofftau, a descent can be made to the Nant Sere. A series of small waterfalls tumbling between steep banks makes this an attractive spot.

On the far side of the stream rise the steep slopes of Bryn Teg, the crest of which curves up gracefully to Cribyn. The climb to the grassy ridgetop is strenuous but not difficult. Once there, a good footpath leads to a final ascent up very steep rocky slopes to the tiny summit of Cribyn. There is no scrambling involved, although this was not the opinion of the walker I heard warning two people about to descend, 'Be careful, that's a real scramble.' His companions nodded, and the two recipients of this advice set off looking quite nervous. I am sure they were surprised at the ease of the descent.

From Cribyn there is an excellent view across Cwm Sere to the rocky north-east face of Pen y Fan. This 120m (400ft) cliff is the biggest in the Beacons and very distinctive, with the red sandstone strata standing out against the green grassy ledges and dark vertical gullies. To the south, the green slopes fall away more gently. Also on the summit of Cribyn, as on Pen y Fan and Corn Du, are the faint remains of bronze-age cairns.

A steep eroded path leads down from Cribyn to the marshy col between the two. Just north of the path, on the edge of Craig Cwm Sere, there are startling views down greasy, vertigo-inducing gullies to the floor of the cwm.

A short pull leads up to Pen y Fan, a perfect name as it means 'Top of the Beacons'. Near the summit the heavily eroded path has been repaired with a staircase of sandstone flags. The views are extensive, with distant hills spread round the horizon beyond a chequer-board of small fields. Identifiable to the east are the Black Mountains, with the distinctive Sugar Loaf prominent. The most impressive view is close to hand, however: the great pyramid of the north face of Cribyn, a peak that looks far steeper than it seemed when walking over it.

Half a kilometre to the west lies the summit of Corn Du, the third of the major Beacons tops. Even if you are descending north from Pen y Fan I would recommend going out and back to Corn Du (the name means Black Horn) for the views of Pen y Fan and down into the glacial hollow of Cwm Llwch.

Back on Pen y Fan there is a break in the summit crags directly north of the trig point, down which an easy scramble leads to the long ridge of Cefn Cwm Llwch which parallels Bryn Teg to the east. The walk down the ridge, easy once the initial scramble is over, gives good views into the deep cwms on either side and, particularly in the lower section, back to the cliffs at the head of Cwm Sere and the rugged summits of Pen y Fan and Cribyn.

At its north end the ridge broadens and splits into two spurs. To reach Cwm Gwdi, descend by the stream between the two or continue over the eastern one, Allt Ddu, keeping to the left-hand side.

TRAVERSING THE CARNEDDAU

*Excellent walking terrain, ideally suited to fast movers
who like to traverse several summits in a day.*

Steve Ashton, *Hill Walking.in Snowdonia*

Start/finish:	Aber to Llyn Ogwen
Summits:	Foel-fras 942m (3,091ft), Garnedd Uchaf 926m (3,038ft), Foel Grach 976m (3,202ft), Carnedd Llywelyn 1,064m (3,491ft), Yr Elen 962m (3,156ft), Carnedd Dafydd 1044m (3,412ft), Penyrole-wen 978m (3,209ft)
Distance:	21km (13miles)
Navigation:	Difficult
Terrain:	Moderate
Winter:	Difficult
Map:	Harveys 1:25,000 Superwalker: Snowdonia North. OS 1:25,000 Outdoor Leisure 16 and 17: Snowdonia – Conwy Valley & Snowdon areas

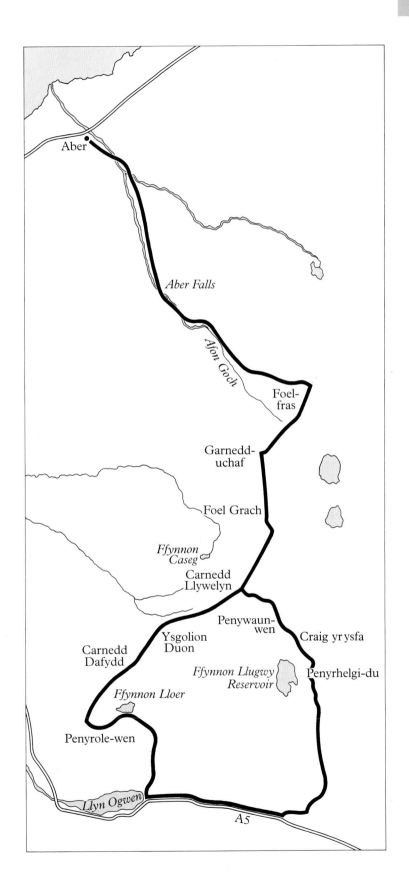

Aber

Aber Falls

Afon Goch

Foel-fras

Garnedd-uchaf

Foel Grach

Ffynnon Caseg

Carnedd Llywelyn

Penywaun-wen

Ysgolion Duon

Craig yr ysfa

Carnedd Dafydd

Ffynnon Llugwy Reservoir

Penyrhelgi-du

Ffynnon Lloer

Penyrole-wen

Llyn Ogwen

A5

Left: *Carnedd Dafydd rising above a cloud inversion.*

The Carneddau are the northernmost summits in Snowdonia National Park, forming a great wedge of high land from the Ogwen valley in the south to the coastal town of Conwy in the north. And high they are, for here lies the largest area of land over 915m (3,000ft) south of the Scottish Highlands. The hills are massive whalebacks with flat tops and long, wide grassy ridges, making for easy walking. Once you are up there, that is, as the slopes rising to the summits are steep and massive cliff-rimmed cwms cut deep into the mountainsides. Rather than having a kinship with the rock peaks just to the south, the Carneddau share many features with the Cairngorms far to the north.

Seven of the 15 915m (3,000ft) hills in Wales are in the Carneddau, and there are 11 other summits over 610m (2,000ft). Carnedd Llywelyn, the highest peak, is also the third highest in Wales, while Carnedd Dafydd is the fourth. They are probably named after the Celtic princes of Wales, Llywelyn the Great (1194–1240) who had a court at Aber on the coast just north of the range, and his successor David.

The structure of the range is relatively simple. A central ridge, bitten into by massive cwms, runs south-west to north-east from Penyrole-wen above Llyn Ogwen to little-known Tal y Fan, the most northerly 610m (2,000ft) summit in Wales, above the Conwy valley. From this main ridge a series of branch ridges run out in all directions. There are a large number of possible high-level walks linking the various summits, either by circular horseshoe routes round the heads of the cwms or up one ridge and down another. The classic route, though, traverses the range from end to end over six of the seven highest summits. The seventh, Yr Elen, lies out on a spur and can also be visited easily.

This walk is excellent whichever way you go but, after several traverses in either direction, I think north to south is by far the best way. This is because you start on the coast, climb gradually into the hills and then head south with the heart of Snowdonia laid out in front of you, to finish with a descent to Llyn Ogwen below the magnificent Glyders. It is a superb way to enter Snowdonia and I have begun several multi-day trips with this route.

Although comprised of rolling, grassy hills rather than rock peaks like those to the south, the Carneddau should not be underestimated. There is little shelter on the high ridges and the featureless terrain makes navigation difficult in mist, while the steep headwalls of many of the cwms means you cannot descend just anywhere.

I learned how serious these hills can be late one March, when a party of five of us set out to traverse the tops to Ogwen. On the coast the weather was hot and still, and we began with sleeves rolled up and socks rolled down. However, by the time we reached 915m (3,000ft) a cold wind had us donning jackets, gloves and hats. To the north-west dark clouds were rolling in off the sea and soon we were shrouded in mist, the wind was blowing us along and icy sleet was hammering down. Just before the summit of Foel Grach we decided that to carry on in the worsening storm would be crazy, so we dropped down into Cwm Eigiau and made camp on what seemed a sheltered spot. Just to the south the great cliff of Craig yr ysfa rose into the mist, its gullies packed with snow. The storm did not leave our camp alone for long. After dark the wind picked up speed and roared down the mountainside in a series of incredible gusts, shaking the tents (one in fact collapsed during the night) and making sleep impossible.

Between the gusts there would be a sudden calm, and then we would hear the roar of the next one as it came down the cwm. Dawn came with torrential rain, so we abandoned any thought of climbing back up to the Carneddau tops and splashed on down to Capel Curig. The ground was sodden, the sky was sodden and I was sodden. It is possibly the wettest I have ever felt.

If you want to traverse all the peaks from Tal y Fan south then the walk can be started from Llanfairfechan, where there is a railway station, or from the Conwy valley. However, the most enjoyable and scenic route starts from Aber (Abergwyngregyn on the Harveys map), not far west along the coast from Llanfairfechan. The initial walk is through pleasant woods on the well-used path leading south to impressive Aber Falls, the highest in Wales, where the Afon Goch tumbles over 30m (100ft) down the cliffs. The Celtic name, Rhaeadr-Fawr, means simply Big Waterfall. Continuing up the beautiful Afon Goch valley the route, now pathless, climbs through two hanging valleys to the head of Cwm yr Afon Goch. An easy ascent of the slopes to the east leads to the first summit, Foel-fras. The Carneddau open up now, and the walking is glorious as the hills

On the Carneddau approaching Carnedd Dafydd.

rise in height and the scenery grows increasingly more rugged and mountainous.

Heading south, Garnedd Uchaf and Foel Grach are easily crossed. Deep craggy cwms lie to either side, that to the north of Yr Elen containing the little lake of Ffynnon Caseg – the Mare's Well or Spring, that to the east of Carnedd Llywelyn Ffynnon Llyfant – the Frog's Well. Soon after these are passed the summit of Carnedd Llywelyn is reached. The view from here is tremendous, both close by and to the horizon. Southwards the spiky Glyders draw the eye, while just across Cwm Pen-llafar to the west the sheer cliffs of Ysgolion Duon – the Black Ladders – abut the summit of Carnedd Dafydd. Yr Elen, out to the north-west and with views out to sea, can be ascended easily from here and then the corner cut on the return to the ridge leading to Carnedd Dafydd.

The going is rockier now and the ridge narrower. In sunny weather it is all a joy – as long as you do not wear too many clothes, that is. I remember once sitting just below the summit of Carnedd Dafydd having a snack when a line of walkers marched past, obviously an organized party, all wearing thick breeches, sweaters and windproof jackets and carrying large packs. They looked grim and serious and were dripping with sweat for it was a hot, windless day. Envious glances were cast at my shorts and T-shirt, and my smile and greeting were not returned. Overheating can be as serious as getting too cold and it certainly does not make for enjoyable walking.

The last section of the ridge leads from Carnedd Dafydd to Penyrole-wen,

a walk dominated by the view ahead to the Glyders, especially the jagged wedge of Tryfan that looks like a dinosaur carved out of rock. Penyrole-wen (the name means Hill of the White Light) looms over the Ogwen valley and it is easy to see that any descent on this side must be steep. The direct route via the south ridge is loose and relentless as it drops 610m (2,000ft) in 1½km (1 mile) without a break on an eroded scree path. However, there is an easier way down the east ridge to the Afon Lloer and then beside this stream to the east end of Llyn Ogwen. There is a short section of easy scrambling near the top of the ridge, however, and this could be hard to find in poor visibility. The lake below the ridge is called Ffynnon Lloer, the Spring of the Moon, presumably linked to the Hill of the White Light above.

A variant route from Carnedd Llywelyn, better in some respects than that described above although it misses out the last two high tops, descends at first easily and then by a short scramble south-east to Bwlch Eryl Farchog and the top of Craig yr ysfa, down which you can peer at the pinnacles and great slabs of rock that make up this massive cliff. A narrow rock ridge with some exciting situations leads up to the 833m (2,733ft) summit of Penyrhelgi-du – the Hill of the Black Hound. The south ridge of this hill, Y Braich, leads down to the A5 about 3½km (2 ¼ miles) east of Llyn Ogwen. The lake below the summit Ffynnon Llugwy, the Well of Clear Water, is in fact a reservoir. The ugly tarmac road that runs up to it – an insult to the hills – could be used for a quick descent, but it would be a poor way to end a superb mountain day.

WALK 4

THE GLYDERS AND TRYFAN

*Sudden clearings in the swirling cloud play tricks with
perspective and the rocks appear gigantic.*

John & Anne Nuttall, *The Mountains of England and Wales*

Start/finish: Llyn Ogwen
Summits: Tryfan 916m (3,002ft), Glyder Fach 994m
(3,261ft), Glyder Fawr 999m (3,278ft)
Distance: 8km (5 miles)
Navigation: Moderate
Terrain: Difficult
Winter: Very difficult
Map: Harveys 1:25,000 Superwalker: Snowdonia
North. OS 1:25,000 Outdoor Leisure 17:
Snowdonia – Snowdon area

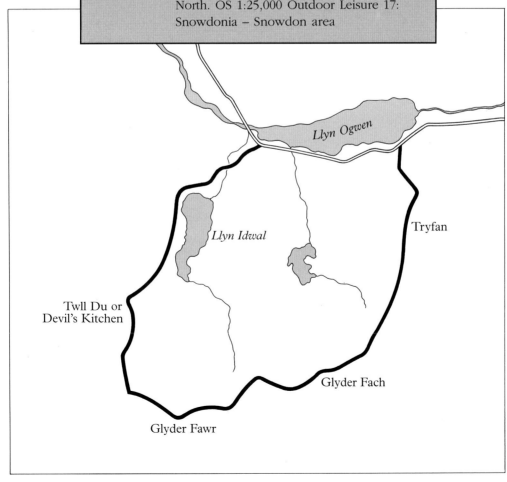

A complex tangle of huge cliffs, pinnacled ridges, deep cwms and mountain lakes, the Glyders have a presence far greater than the small area they cover would seem to warrant. But in those few square kilometres are to be found crammed what is arguably the finest mountain landscape in England and Wales and one that ranks with the best in the Scottish Highlands. This is country for those who love steep rock scenery that changes with almost every step.

The range is named for the two highest hills, Glyder Fawr and Glyder Fach, but is dominated by the great wedge of Tryfan, as near to a perfect rock peak as can be imagined. There is

Tryfan and Glyder Fawr seen across Cwm Idwal.

no gentle side to Tryfan, no easy way up. Indeed, it is often said that Tryfan is the only peak south of the Highlands that cannot be climbed with your hands in your pockets, although some will undoubtedly have done this. Tryfan means Three Tops, an obvious name when the peak is seen side on. Glyder has a prosaic meaning as well. It means

'pile' or 'heap', a reference presumably to the random collection of boulders found on each summit. Fawr and Fach mean 'big' and 'little', so we have the Big Pile and the Little Pile. I think the Celtic sounds better! Although collectively known as the Glyders, this is an Anglicization. It should really be Glyderau.

The steep slopes and preponderance of rock make this a superb region for the scrambler, as well as a major rock climbing area. Even the walking routes are rough and stony. Of the many possibilities, the round of Tryfan and the two Glyders is one of the best. It includes two superb but relatively easy scrambles, the North Ridge of Tryfan and Bristly Ridge on Glyder Fach, the excellent high-level walk from Glyder Fach to Glyder Fawr, and a descent beside the Devil's Kitchen to Cwm Idwal, one of the most impressive cirques in the British mountains. This is as perfect as you can get. Lying directly above the A5 trunk road, however, the whole route is easily accessible and therefore very popular. Very early or, in summer only, late starts are a way to avoid the worst of the crowds as well as to get the best light.

It is not a route for wet, windy weather, as I found on my first two attempts to climb the North Ridge of Tryfan. Torrential rain pouring down the rocks persuaded me to turn back the first time, while my second effort was abandoned when thunder crashed overhead and lightning flashed all around. The third try was the lucky one, although the top was in mist and heavy rain on the descent caused us to continue back down to Ogwen rather than going on to the Glyders. Further visits have also mostly been in wet weather – including one late-April weekend when it snowed down to valley level and we never got further than a few feet up Tryfan. A week earlier we had been sunbathing outside the tent at Stickle Tarn in the Lake District! In fact, the weather has been wet and windy on most of my visits to Snowdonia. I am assured it is not always like that. I have been over Tryfan and the Glyders in clear weather once, however. In a strange way it felt quite disappointing.

Tryfan's North Ridge begins not far above the valley floor and continues unbroken to the summit. However, it is not as steep or difficult as it appears from below, being quite wide – more of a buttress than a ridge – and with the short sections of steep scrambling interspersed with gentler sections where you can walk. Over the years a path has developed on the east side some distance below the crest for those who really do not like scrambling.

The central and highest summit is topped by two large stone monoliths known as Adam and Eve. Some people like to jump from one to the other – which is fine if you have a good sense of balance and if you are not easily intimidated by the sheer drops to the side. From the tiny summit a rather easier scramble over large boulders leads down the South Ridge to the col of Bwlch Tryfan. The easiest going is on the west side.

Above Bwlch Tryfan, Bristly Ridge rears up in a great spine of pinnacles and rocks. If you do not fancy another scramble, there is a path from the col running south-east up the scree, past the ridge and round the head of Cwm Tryfan, to the broad east shoulder of Glyder Fach. The exciting way up, though, is by the ridge which, like the North Ridge of Tryfan, is not as hard as it looks from below. The scramble ends not far from a famous balanced rock known as the Cantilever, just beyond which lies the jumble of scattered boulders that make up the summit of Glyder Fach. To the south the Snowdon massif dominates the view, while ahead lie the strange rock splinters known as Castell y Gwynt – the Castle of the Winds.

The Glyders ridge in winter.

Mountain walking in thick mist is always a slightly strange experience but here it is positively eerie, with weirdly shaped rocks looming up unexpectedly. Perhaps due to the weather conditions I have usually experienced here, I have always felt a sense of tension and uncertainty on the Glyders, a feeling that the mountains are unfriendly.

One occasion when the mountains definitely were unfriendly (or at least that is how it seemed – logically I know that lumps of rock have no feelings or senses) followed the storm in the Carneddau I described in the last walk. Following our retreat to Capel Curig, two of us decided to walk over the Glyders to Llyn Ogwen. The rest of the party opted, sensibly, to follow the old road in the valley. At first the weather was clear and progress good. The first hint of a change came just before Castell y Gwynt, when I fell through a hole in a patch of snow and cracked my right shin on a rock on the way down. Shortly after this we encountered a slope of hard, icy snow. Foolishly we set off across it with our ice axes still strapped to our rucksacks. A look down the long steep slopes to the south persuaded us to stop and carefully unbuckle our axes. While doing this my companion lost one of his mitts, whipped away by the wind which had begun a short while before and was strengthening rapidly.

Dark clouds were now rushing in from the west, so we pushed on rapidly over Glyder Fawr as rain began to fall. The steep slope down to Llyn y Cwn was covered with a thin layer of hard snow and we needed to kick steps to descend this. Or at least Steve did: my right leg, now throbbing and painful, had no power in it and I could not kick secure footholds. Steve had to cut steps for me, which slowed us down considerably. By now it was raining

heavily and dusk was closing in (it was late March), so we rushed on down the path into Cwm Idwal and along the A5 to the campsite where we were to meet the rest of the party. The rain hammered down, but we were in so much of a hurry that I did not bother to don waterproofs over my polycotton windproof jacket and acrylic/wool shirt. By the time we arrived at the site I was soaked to the skin and shivering violently. I found I could not pitch my tent and had to be rewarmed in a sleeping bag in another tent while my friends pitched mine. The mistakes that led to this were of course mine and could have had the same results any-where, but it is perhaps not surprising that I am a little wary of the Glyders.

When the weather is better the walk between the two Glyders is tremendous, with great views across Llanberis Pass to the Snowdon Horseshoe. The paths down to Llyn y Cwn – the Pool of the Dog – are loose and eroded but not difficult. Heading for the edge of the cliffs to the north, the route now descends a diagonal ramp through the crags that emerges at the base of the Devil's Kitchen – Twll Du in Welsh, which means the Black Hole – a dark gash nearly 305m (1,000ft) high, down which tumbles a ribbon of a stream. Twll Du lies at the back of magnificent Cwm Idwal which is a designated nature reserve on account of the alpine flora found here. To the right are the famous Idwal Slabs, first climbed in 1895 and still popular today. The vertical face here soars nearly 500m (1,650ft) to the summit slopes of Glyder Fawr.

A final descent on a rocky path leads from Llyn Idwal to the west end of Llyn Ogwen. There is a very welcome café here and also Idwal Cottage, one of the first youth hostels, which opened in 1931.

THE CLOGWYN Y PERSON ARETE

CRIB-Y-DDYSGL AND CRIB GOCH

A region that has the grandeur and dark glamour of the Gothic. Standing on the summit of Snowdon you feel these bristling mountains as the impregnable fortress they once were, the last stronghold of warriors.

Showell Styles, *Snowdonia National Park*

Start/finish:	Llanberis Pass
Summits:	Crib-y-Ddysgl (Garnedd Ugain) 1,065m (3,493ft), Crib Goch 923m (3,027ft)
Distance:	6½km (4 miles)
Navigation:	Difficult
Terrain:	Very difficult
Winter:	Very difficult
Maps:	Harveys 1:25,000 Superwalker: Snowdonia West. OS 1:25,000 Outdoor Leisure 17: Snowdonia – Snowdon area

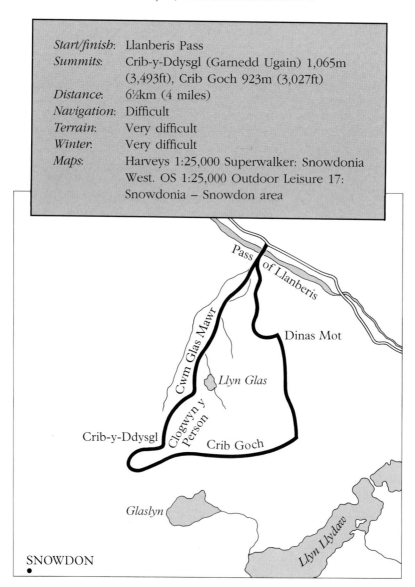

The Llanberis Pass is one of the most spectacular and well-known mountain passes in Britain, with the two most popular mountain massifs in the Snowdonia National Park towering over it: the Glyders to the north and Snowdon itself to the south. What the traveller through the pass actually sees to the south, though, is a wild and craggy bowl backed by the pinnacled ridges of Crib Goch and Crib-y-Ddysgl. This beautiful and complex cirque is called Cwm Glas. Ridges, buttresses and cliffs divide the cwm into many smaller ones higher up but the central one, Cwm Glas Mawr, reaches up to the foot of Crib-y-Ddysgl, to end below the treacherous and loose-looking Clogwyn y Ddysgl cliffs. There are few ways out of the cwm for the walker, but for those with a good head for heights the Clogwyn y Person arete is an exciting route. Those with less of a liking for exposure could instead climb the ridge on the west side of Cwm Glas, a rough walk with a few bits of easy scrambling. This is also a good descent route and the one to choose in bad weather.

The best route, however, is the Clogwyn y Person arete, described by Steve Ashton in *Scrambles in Snowdonia* as 'one of the finest natural lines in the area'. There are few places outside the Cuillin of Skye or the Northern Highlands where you can spend all day in or above a single high valley on rock most of the time. The arete is the ridge dividing upper Cwm Glas from Cwm Uchaf to the east. The rockface below the ridge, Clogwyn y Person – the Parson's Nose – is named on the OS Outdoor Leisure map but not on the Harveys Superwalker sheet.

This is a route for dry, sunny weather and it was on a hot summer morning that three of us, plus a dog, walked up lower Cwm Glas, watching the rock climbers already high on the

walls of Cyrn Las. Impatient to reach the arete, we began scrambling beside the stream that runs down the east side of Cyrn Las (it is easier to keep well left of the stream and walk up the rocky slopes to Llyn Glas). The slabs of warm, rough rock were pleasant to the touch and progress was easy, even Graham's dog Kelly, the least experienced of the group, managing to climb everything.

I find that over-confidence and lack of thought is far more likely on fine sunny days than in bad weather, when there is always an awareness of the possibility of going astray or slipping.

On the Clogwyn y Person arete.

On this occasion I failed to think ahead as, wanting to stay close to the water, I scrambled up a narrow gully in the stream itself. When it became too steep and wet to continue, I attempted the wall on my left. For a short distance it was fine, then suddenly I found myself standing in the pool at the bottom, breathless in the cold spray of water and with grazed legs. The top of my little wall was black with slime and I could see the marks where this had slid off when I put my boots on it. Unhurt but a little shaken, I was pleased to accept a top rope, which enabled me to overcome the greasy rocks.

I should, of course, have noted the nature of the terrain above me before I began to climb, but I had not yet grasped the seriousness of the scramble, and anyway we were not on the 'real' route yet. That all scrambling requires care and attention was a lesson I was able to dwell on as I stood in my cold shower clad only in boots and shorts, waiting for the rope to be thrown down to me.

Back in the sun and warmed up again, I admired the magnificent scenery of upper Cwm Glas. Several tents were pitched here: a superb wild site. A small group of people on a nearby knoll marked a checkpoint for a police mountain marathon that was taking place.

Arriving at the foot of the imposing end of the arete itself, we decided to begin the climb by scrambling up Western Gully, a deep, chockstone-filled groove that separates the arete proper from the blunt buttress of the Parson's Nose that lies at its end. There is a harder route up the side of the nose itself. Initially the scrambling simply consists of heaving yourself over large boulders in the gully bed, but eventually you are pushed out on to ledges on the right wall as the gully becomes steeper and smoother. Here Graham left us, as the vertical sides of the ledges, although not very big, were too much for Kelly.

Route finding is important when scrambling, and I suspect that we made the climb more difficult above the gully than it need have been by our route choice. Certainly we climbed some steep and exposed rocks on the west side of the arete, where we were glad of the rope. We did not mind, however, as it was very enjoyable climbing the grooves and walls in the hot sunshine, with the tiny mountain pools of Llyn Bach and Llyn Glas sparkling on the floor of the cwm below us. The voices of policemen sweating up to their checkpoint echoed across the cwm from rock wall to rock wall.

Eventually we reached the broad crest of the arete. Hauling myself over an overhanging boulder on to a slab, I came face to face with another scrambler hauling himself on to the same slab from a different direction. As his move looked more difficult than mine and the slab was fairly small, I dropped back on to my footholds and let him pass. His companion, rope over shoulder, was just behind and soon followed by another party. Both groups were coming up the arete itself, which suggested we had left the gully too soon, thus increasing the difficulty of the climb.

Once on the arete the difficulties eased, and we put away the rope. As we climbed, the arete narrowed until it was almost a knife edge. Oddly enough, the scrambling is simplest where the arete is sharpest, being almost a walk. This enabled us to appreciate the dramatic views of Crib Goch with its attendant jagged ridges, a line of sharp, white quartz just below the summit reflecting the sunlight. As usual, a steady line of people was heading along the ridge towards Snowdon. Arriving on the ridge not far beneath the summit of Crib-y-Ddysgl was quite a shock. The views of Snowdon and Lliwedd and, far below our feet, the waters of Glaslyn and Llyn Llydaw, were impressive – but the people! Hordes everywhere: grim-faced heavy-booted hikers, some in anoraks, heavy breeches and thick socks despite the hot sun, as if to ensure that everyone knew they were serious hillwalkers, mingled with family parties dressed for a day on the beach and clutching carrier bags. It was all too much, and we quickly abandoned our tentative plan to nip up and down nearby Snowdon and headed directly for Crib Goch instead.

I did not mind, as I dislike the summit of Snowdon – not the mountain itself, you understand, but what has been done to it. Railways and cafés have no place on mountaintops and I hate these ones in particular because of the disappointment they led to early in my walking life, a disappointment that probably helped form the views I now hold about keeping the hills truly wild. I first came here on a school trip at the age of 13. On a cold, wet day we scaled Crib Goch, its rocks dripping with water. A thick mist hung over the mountains, limiting visibility to a few metres. The traverse of the Crib Goch Pinnacles was exciting – this was real mountaineering! Finally, the summit of Snowdon came into view: there was a building on top. We went in, to be overwhelmed by the noise and warmth. A host of train-borne tourists in shorts and T-shirts, skirts and high heels stared at us, dripping with rain and sweat and dressed in old jumpers, torn anoraks

and surplus-store boots, as if we were the ones out of place. I felt a terrible sense of disillusionment. This was not what mountain summits should be like. I wanted a wild, savage remoteness, a feeling of being far from the tameness of civilization. I still do.

The crest of the ridge east down to Bwlch Coch was an airy and invigorating walk. Then we climbed up and around the Pinnacles and along the narrow ridge to the summit of Crib Goch. As the rock was dry and there was no wind we were able to balance along the top of the ridge (in wet and windy weather it is better to stay just below the crest using the top for handholds) – a highly enjoyable way of feeling in tune with the rock, oneself and the mountains.

From the tiny red-rock summit (Crib Goch means Red Comb) we set off down the North Ridge, where we could see Graham and Kelly heading up. A family party heading down the standard route of the East Ridge seemed both puzzled and irritated that we were not doing the same and discussed us loudly as if we weren't there!

A pleasant and narrow ridge in its upper part, the North Ridge does not suffer the huge volumes of traffic found on the other Crib Goch ridges. This is probably because it is not so easy to reach, as access to the lower end is blocked by the mighty walls of Dinas Mot. To avoid this crag we ran down the scree slopes west of the ridge into upper Cwm Uchaf, from where a narrow path led through little crags round the side of Dinas Mot and back to Llanberis Pass.

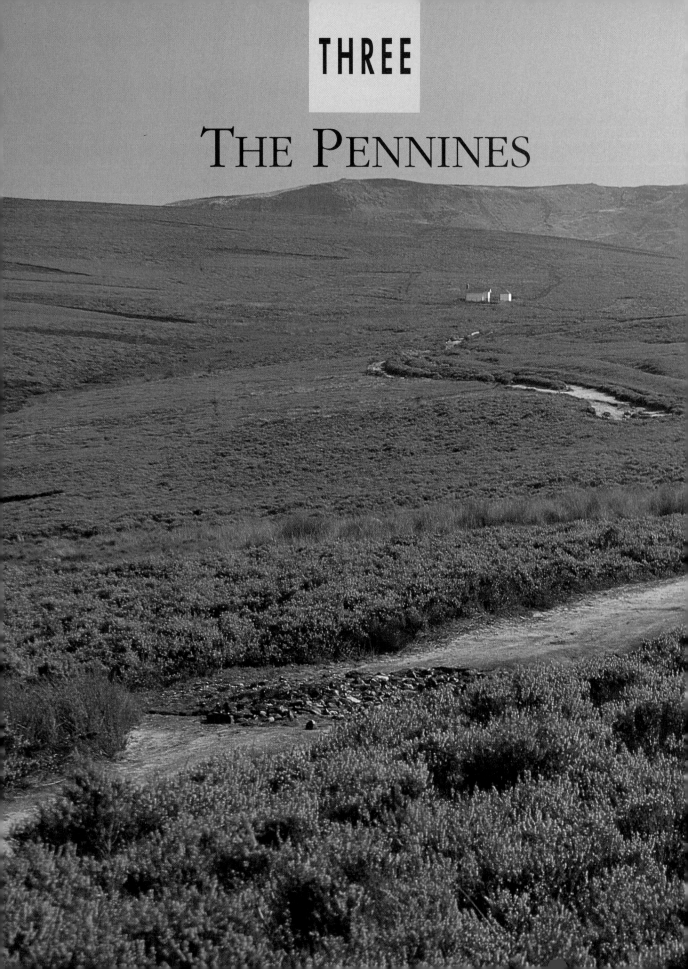

THREE

THE PENNINES

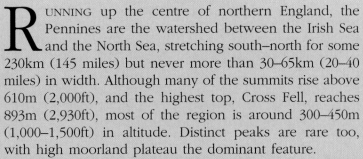

RUNNING up the centre of northern England, the Pennines are the watershed between the Irish Sea and the North Sea, stretching south–north for some 230km (145 miles) but never more than 30–65km (20–40 miles) in width. Although many of the summits rise above 610m (2,000ft), and the highest top, Cross Fell, reaches 893m (2,930ft), most of the region is around 300–450m (1,000–1,500ft) in altitude. Distinct peaks are rare too, with high moorland plateau the dominant feature.

The Pennines are not a single chain or range of hills, there being several distinct geographical areas. In the south, the White Peak consists of a limestone plateau at around 305m (1,000ft), dissected by deep and impressive cliff-lined, gorge-like dales. The name Peak, by the way, comes from the Old English 'peac' which means a hill of any shape, rather than the pointed summit we mean by the word today. There are few peaks in the Peak District.

North of the White Peak the high country of the Pennines really starts, with the 610m (2,000ft) peat plateaux of the Dark Peak. Outcrops of millstone grit along the edges of these boggy uplands and deep stream-cut rocky ravines, known as cloughs, are the most impressive features.

Further north again, the limestone reappears in what is arguably the most attractive area of the Pennines, the Yorkshire Dales, where great whalebacked hills, most notably the Three Peaks, tower over fascinating limestone scenery. Out to the west the Howgill Fells form a link with the Lake District hills.

Finally, at the northern end of the range the peat moorland reappears (it has never really disappeared – there are plenty of bogs in the Dales), although not in so virulent a form as further south. Here, in the Northern Pennines, are the highest and remotest peaks, with rock outcroppings and deep valleys such as High Cup again a main attraction.

There is fine walking throughout the Pennines, especially for those who love wide horizons, big skies and the sight of waves of moorland stretching into the distance. It is a popular region for long-distance challenge walks such as the Derwent Watershed and the Marsden to Edale, both 40km (25 miles) in length. Longest of all is the 400km (250 miles) Pennine Way, although around a quarter of this path, some 100km (60 miles), is actually north of the Pennines.

KINDER SCOUT

*The top of Kinder Scout looks as if it's entirely covered
in the droppings of dinosaurs.*

John Hillaby, *Journey Through Britain*

Start/finish:	Edale village in the Vale of Edale
Summits:	Kinder Scout 636m (2,088ft), Kinder Low 628m (2,060ft). Note that these are not summits in the normal sense of the word!
Distance:	23km (14 miles) for the round of the Kinder edges
Navigation:	Difficult
Terrain:	Difficult
Winter:	Moderate
Maps:	Harveys 1:25,000 Superwalker: Dark Peak North. OS 1:25,000 Outdoor Leisure 1: The Peak District – Dark Peak area

The rain lashed down as I stumbled, cold, wet and weary, down the never-ending rough hillside. Inside my so-called waterproof cagoule, a thin nylon garment purchased in a surplus store, I was soaked. It was November and I was trying to get off Kinder Scout on a dark, wet evening. Where exactly I was I did not know, as I had no torch or compass. All I knew was that I was cold and miserable and wanted to be home and not out here on a storm-blasted hillside with the prospect of a broken leg threatening with every step.

Although I got down safely, I shivered all the way back to Manchester and was laid up with a heavy cold for the next week. I had never heard of it at the time, but I had just had a close brush with hypothermia, the result of becoming too cold, too wet, too tired and too demoralized. This was learning the hard way indeed. For half a dozen years I had gone hillwalking with school parties but, although I had been up many hills in the Peak, the Lakes and North Wales, I had never used a compass or carried a torch, nor learnt much in the way of skills. I left school in love with hillwalking but with no idea how to do it safely. Now a student in Manchester, I was learning on the moors of the Dark Peak.

Having survived that storm on Kinder I bought a torch, though not yet a compass, then repeated the episode a few weeks later. This time I learnt to reverse the batteries in my torch so that it could not turn on accidentally in the rucksack, and also to carry spare batteries.

Since those early misadventures I have walked on Kinder many times summer and winter, and run all over it on a mountain marathon. I have never been badly lost again, but my respect for this southern end of the Pennines has not diminished.

Kinder Scout is a vast moorland plateau covering some 13sq km (5sq miles) and averaging 610m (2,000ft) in height. There are no summits as such, the high point (or points – the OS give three of equal height) being only marginally higher than the surroundings. These lie in a sea of chocolate brown, glutinous peat cut by deep water channels called groughs. Much of the peat is bare, the rest covered with cotton grass and other acid-resistant plants like heather, bilberry and crow-berry. Walking over this terrain involves lurching from tussock to tussock, and ploughing up and down the sodden sides of the groughs knee-deep and more in semi-liquid peat. Only after a long drought or, best of all, when the ground is frozen hard, is it easy to walk across Kinder Scout. Navigation is always problematical, as paths are non-existent even though the Pennine Way crosses the plateau. If in doubt, walking north or south in as straight a line as possible until you reach the edge is the best way to escape.

The finest walking is not in the featureless, viewless heart of Kinder Scout, however, but on the rim, where the forces of erosion have laid bare the underlying millstone grit – whose dark colour is the reason this is known as the Dark Peak – and sculpted it into strange monoliths and contorted towers, many with their own names: the Wool Packs, Pym Chair, Noe Stool. As well as these curious rock formations, there are extensive views. North and east the high peat moorlands continue across Ashop Clough and the Woodlands and Derwent Valleys, while to the south lies the Mam Tor ridge that marks the divide between the Dark Peak and the airy, light limestone scenery of the White Peak. Westwards lie the snaking roads and faint tower blocks of Manchester and its satellites, often under a haze of

Previous pages:
The approach to Kinder Scout from the west.

smoke. Also on the edge of the plateau is the trig point of Kinder Low, just 3m (10ft) lower than the high points out in the peat morass. If you want a summit, this one is easy to reach. I'm happy with it!

Kinder Scout is important in the history of hillwalking as it was here that many of the struggles for access to the hills took place, culminating in the famous Mass Trespass of 1932 which saw five ramblers end up in prison. Only after the National Parks and Access to the Countryside Act of 1949, and the setting up of the Peak District National Park in 1951, were access agreements negotiated with the landowners. Until then, these moors were the exclusive preserve of grouse shooters and keepers were employed to keep walkers off. Even today there is still no right to roam on the Pennine moors (some are still closed to walkers) as access agreements can be withdrawn – as they sometimes are temporarily for grouse shooting or because of fire risk. This I consider an invidious position, as I have never recognized the right of any individual to claim exclusive ownership of wild land (I actually think the whole idea is nonsense). I have always gone wherever I wanted, but I am not happy having to trespass and would like to see the freedom to roam on uncultivated land enshrined in law. Whenever I walk on Kinder I think of those who campaigned for years for the right to do so. We owe them much.

Coming from the same tradition as the access campaign is Britain's first and most famous long-distance path, the Pennine Way, which begins (or finishes) at Edale and crosses Kinder Scout from south to north. The idea for the Way

Looking down on Kinder Reservoir from Kinder Scout.

was first mooted in an article in the *Daily Express* by Tom Stephenson in 1935. At the time this was a startling and radical idea, as much of the proposed route was across private shooting estates. Thirty years later the Way was officially opened and since then many thousands of walkers have set off across Kinder Scout, their hearts set on reaching Kirk Yetholm, some 400km (250 miles) to the north.

The best walk on Kinder is a complete round of the edges. This can be started anywhere, but the classic place is the village of Edale to the south. Despite its immense popularity Edale is a relatively unspoilt, attractive hamlet with a café, campsite and two good pubs. I would suggest doing the round clockwise, so that the popular western end of the plateau where the Pennine Way runs is walked first, leaving the less frequented, wilder eastern edges for the end of the day. The walk is good in either direction, though, and there are many escape routes down the numerous cloughs if bad weather closes in, as in fact it all too often does.

The route leaves Edale by the famous log footbridge across Grinds Brook that marks the start of the Pennine Way, and then follows that footpath across pleasant meadows and up increasingly steep and rocky Grindsbrook Clough. On reaching the plateau edge, we turn westwards and stay with the Pennine Way to the head of Crowden Clough. Here the Way plunges into the peat as it heads northwards across the centre of Kinder. The edges route continues west on easier, firmer ground past Pym Chair and Noe Stool to Edale Rocks, where it joins the alternative Pennine Way route that comes up Jacob's Ladder to the south. The Kinder Low trig point is soon reached and then the clear path is followed along the rim to the Downfall, where the Kinder River drops some 30m (100ft) off the plateau.

A miniature amphitheatre ringed by gritstone cliffs, this is a fine spot by any mountain standards. In strong winds the water is blown back up in the air in a great plume: I have been soaked crossing the river well back from the edge when this inverted cascade comes down. In hard winters the Downfall freezes into a mass of white ice, spectacular to see and a major attraction to winter climbers. There is often an ice cave behind the frozen fringe of spear-like giant icicles. Although the name Kinder Scout is now applied to the whole plateau, it originally meant just the area around the Downfall as it is apparently a corruption of the Celtic/Norse Cin dwr Scwd or Kyndwr Skuti, meaning Hill of the Waterfall or Water over the Edge.

The two branches of the Pennine Way come together at the Downfall and we stick with the long-distance path as we head to the northwest corner of Kinder. Here the Way drops down to Ashop Head and continues north through the bogs of Mill Hill and Moss Castle. Our route leaves it to go eastwards along the northern rim of Kinder, known as The Edge, above Ashop Clough to the rocks of Fairbrook Naze. Here there is another abrupt change of direction to south-west, where the Fair Brook has cut deeply into the plateau. Once round the head of this stream it is eastwards again along Seal Edge, round the head of Blackden Brook, and along Blackden Edge to Crookstone Knoll, which marks the far eastern corner of Kinder. The plateau is at its narrowest here, so the route turns south-west almost immediately, crosses the head of Jaggers Clough and then runs westwards past Ringing Roger, Nether Tor and Upper Tor back to Grindsbrook Clough.

BLEAKLOW

*An inhospitable wilderness over which progress on foot
is very arduous. Nobody loves Bleaklow. All who get
on it are glad to get off.*

A. Wainwright, *Pennine Way Companion*

Start/finish:	Crowden in Longdendale or Old Glossop
Summits:	Bleaklow Head 628m (2,060ft), Bleaklow Stones 627m (2,056ft), Higher Shelf Stones 621m (2,036ft)
Distance:	14km (9 miles) for both routes
Navigation:	Difficult
Terrain:	Difficult
Winter:	Moderate
Maps:	Harveys 1:25,000 Superwalker: Dark Peak North. OS 1:25,000 Outdoor Leisure 1: The Peak District – Dark Peak area

*Crossing Bleaklow
in February.*

Bleaklow, like Kinder Scout, is a high gritstone plateau covered by a deep blanket of peat. If anything, it is even more desolate on top, as unbroken peat moorland stretches out in every direction. The edges are less defined than those of Kinder, although in places there are small crags and tors. There are good walks here, however, including an excellent rock scramble, something rare in the Dark Peak.

To the north of Bleaklow lies Longdendale, a heavily industrialized valley containing a series of reservoirs, a disused railway line, a main road and electricity pylons. It is hardly an attractive place for walkers, though it was probably once beautiful, but many come here because of the proximity of Bleaklow and, to the north, Black Hill. The Pennine Way crosses the valley too. At Crowden, once a flourishing village, there is a youth hostel in a row of old terraced cottages, and a good campsite.

The scramble referred to above lies on the north side of Bleaklow, so Crowden is a good starting point. From there the Pennine Way can be followed west through some fields and then south across the Torside Reservoir dam. Here it can be left for a walk along either the B6105 road or the old railway track to the bottom of Wildboar Clough (there are places to park cars).

Wildboar Clough is a narrow ravine down which a stream cascades over a series of gritstone steps. The scrambling is mostly easy and the harder sections can usually be avoided, although sometimes the steep diversions up loose, peaty slopes with heather as handholds seem more precarious than the rock they avoid. At times pools have to be edged round or waded across, and the stream is always in close proximity. This is not a climb to do after heavy rain, unless you like a soaking and are happy climbing slippery rock. In deep snow and when the stream is frozen it would be much more difficult – more a mountaineering route than a walk on which you use your hands – although I did once climb the clough in January when there was ice on the rocks and the water was bitterly cold. It is best in dry conditions when it is an interesting way on to Bleaklow.

The lower part of the clough is the steepest and narrowest. Around 450m (1,500ft) it starts to become less of a ravine and more of a moorland stream. After another 90m (300ft) of ascent the stream, now flowing in a peat grough rather than a rock canyon, can be left for an arduous slog through the quagmire south-east to Bleaklow Head, marked by a large pile of stones. Just to the south are the Wain Stones, often called The Kiss due to the likeness of the boulders to two heads. From the summit the Pennine Way, renovated with stone flags, can be taken back down to Longdendale. A more interesting route is to descend into Torside Clough rather than follow the Way along its western edge. It is mostly a walk, with bits of scrambling in places, but the stream and the rocks make it more enjoyable than the dreary moor above.

Masochists may want to visit Bleaklow's other summit, Bleaklow Stones, a collection of bizarre weathered gritstone boulders which lie some 2km (1¼ miles) to the east of Bleaklow Head. The featureless route is marked by a line of posts, but though this makes the navigation easier it does nothing for the going, which is arduous, especially when it is wet.

My second-favourite route on Bleaklow, and one that I walked frequently when living in Manchester as it was only a short bus journey away, is that from the village of Old Glossop to the west. This climbs slowly past wooded Shire Hill to follow the gritstone slab-paved track known as Doctor's Gate beside Shelf Brook, to join the Pennine Way just north of the Snake Road. Doctor's Gate is a medieval packhorse route which follows the line of the Roman road that ran from Glossop to Castleton and is probably named after a Dr John Talbot, a vicar in Glossop from 1494 to 1550. From the junction the Pennine Way can be followed directly to Bleaklow Head, but a diversion to Higher Shelf Stones to the west is well worthwhile for the views across Bleaklow to Derwent Edge and south to Kinder Scout. An alternative way to reach Higher Shelf Stones is from Doctor's Gate via the cloughs or slopes to the north. The descent from Bleaklow Head can be made via Dowstone Clough and Yellowslack Brook. Near the top of the latter are some crags which the local farmer attempted to blow up in the 1960s to discourage rock climbers from visiting them. Some damage was done but eventually the Peak District National Park authorities negotiated access agreements for the area.

PEN-Y-GHENT

The view is outstandingly good.

A. Wainwright, *Walks in Limestone Country*

Start/finish: Horton-in-Ribblesdale

Summits: Pen-y-ghent 694m (2,277ft), Plover Hill
680m (2,231ft)

Distance: 12km (7½ miles)

Navigation: Easy

Terrain: Easy

Winter: Moderate

Maps: OS 1:25,000 Outdoor Leisure 2 and 30:
Yorkshire Dales – Western area and
Northern & Central areas

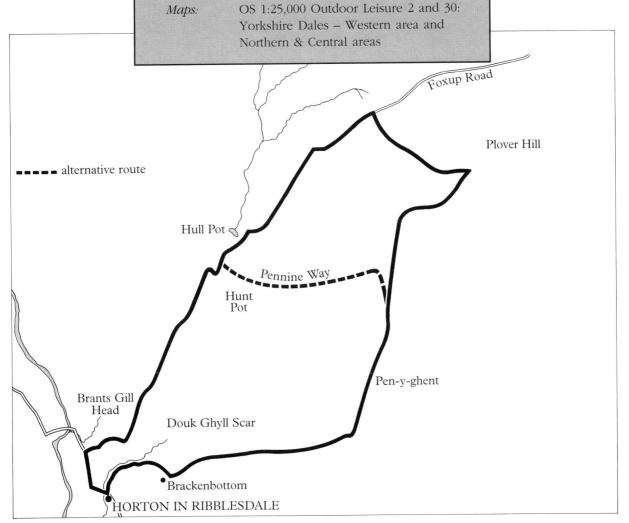

- - - - - alternative route

Foxup Road

Plover Hill

Hull Pot

Pennine Way

Hunt Pot

Pen-y-ghent

Brants Gill Head

Douk Ghyll Scar

Brackenbottom

HORTON IN RIBBLESDALE

Pen-y-ghent is one of the famous Three Peaks of Yorkshire, the others being Ingleborough (see Walk 9) and Whernside (the Ribblesdale Whernside that is, not the Wharfedale Great Whernside). Although the lowest in height of the three, Pen-y-ghent is the only one that lies on the Pennine watershed between the Irish Sea and the North Sea, the waters of the other two running west. Unlike most of the Pennines, the summits in the Dales are distinct hills split by deep, wide valleys rather than linked by high moors. This gives them a great attraction to walkers, as each hill has a character of its own.

The well-known 37km (23 miles) Three Peaks Walk, first walked in 1887 by two teachers from Giggleswick, Canon J.R. Wynne-Edwards and D.R. Smith, links the three but is so popular, and so used by groups for challenge walks and for annual fell and cyclo-cross races, that severe erosion to the terrain has resulted. Over the last decade much repair work has been done. The restored footpaths look a bit artificial and new, but they should weather into their surroundings like the packhorse routes of old. If their con-struction results in a firm, long-lasting, erosion-resistant path then perhaps the Three Peaks Walk can be recommended again, but for now it should be avoided. The route misses out the best approaches to Ingleborough anyway.

But back to Pen-y-ghent. In some ways a typical Pennine whaleback, Pen-y-ghent is more distinctive than similar hills due to the prominent two tiers of its southern face, which give the hill a profile often described as being like that of a crouching lion, although I find this a bit fanciful myself. I do not like comparing hills to animals anyway, so let us just say that Pen-y-ghent is easily identified from afar by the two steps on its southern side. The lower step

consists of pale Yoredale limestone, while the top one is dark gritstone. The break between the two rock types is quite abrupt and very noticeable on the ascent of the hill.

The unusual name is Celtic and derives from either Pen y cant, which means Hill of the Border or Rim, or Pen y gwynt, which means Hill of the Winds. Both would be appropriate, as the hill borders Ribblesdale and it can certainly be very windy on the summit.

Pen-y-ghent is inextricably linked with Horton-in-Ribblesdale at its foot, both because it dominates the hamlet and because the Pennine Way descends here after crossing the summit, giving weary walkers a chance to relax in its pubs and the well-known Pen-y-ghent Café, where they serve pint mugs of tea and coffee.

Of the many approaches to Pen-y-ghent, my favourite is the one from Brackenbottom just outside Horton, as this gives an excellent view of the dramatic profile of the hill. The extensively repaired path climbs swiftly eastwards up the hillside to join the Pennine Way just south of the rock steps. These and the intervening boulder field are steep but easy to negotiate, although the lower limestone one can be very slippery when wet. Pennine Way walkers with heavy packs may find it awkward, too.

Certainly I did on my first Pennine Way walk in the 1970s. In those days, external pack frames that towered over your head were popular with backpackers and I was proud of my American model, which bore the surreal combined name of Ponderosa for the packbag and Astral Cruiser for the frame. (Oddly enough, my current internal frame backpack, also American, bears the name Astralplane.) Climbing the wet, greasy limestone of the lower tier in the rain, I found the tall frame

Pen-y-ghent and the River Ribble.

banging me on the back of the head and forcing my face into the slope. I ended up virtually crawling up the steepest bit. Perhaps such experiences are one reason that these packs did not remain popular for long in Britain. A more positive aspect of the limestone terraces on Pen-y-ghent is that in spring the rare purple saxifrage flourishes here, its bright flowers bringing a touch of colour to the scene.

Although the climb can be done in an hour or so, this is still a high mountain and the weather can be wild. One of my first visits was with a university hillwalking club. The weather was fairly cloudy when we set off and by the time we reached the start of the rock steps the rain was lashing down, the wind was threatening to blow us off

the mountain and visibility was down to a few metres. Wisely, the group leader opted to return to Horton. However, a few of us were determined to reach the top and pressed on, to stagger over the summit and stumble down the wet, muddy path back to Horton. The whole hillside was running with water, and distinguishing the path from the rest of the sodden terrain was surprisingly difficult. Map and compass were required to keep us on course.

Once above the rock steps, a wall leads across the peaty summit to the trig point. On a clear day the view is extensive, with the other Dales tops visible all around while away to the north-west the southern Lakeland fells draw the eye. Rather than lose the views by descending immediately,

I would suggest staying high and walking north for 1.6km (1 mile) or so to the large cairn on Plover Hill. From here you can descend north-westwards to the Foxup path and follow this south to Horton. Alternatively, you can return to where the Pennine Way starts its descent, just north of the line of small crags that run along the western edge of Pen-y-ghent, and follow the long-distance path down into Horton. The advantage of this route, which is also the one to take if Plover Hill is not visited, is that it passes close to Hunt and Hull Pots, both of which are worth taking in. These lie at 400m (1,300ft), where limestone appears on the surface again and the streams that run down from the summit plateau vanish into the ground.

The scenery of the limestone country of the Dales is distinctive and unique, a wonderful and strange world of pale cliffs and pinnacles, dry valleys and coves, disappearing streams and resurgences, potholes and sinks, all formed by a combination of glaciation and the slow dissolution of the lime-stone by the weak acids found in rain. Where the limestone lies on the surface, as in much of the south-west Dales, rainwater cuts channels into it to form the large limestone pavements found throughout the area, or so one theory claims, although exactly how these surprisingly regular pavements are formed is not known for certain, nor why large flat areas of limestone are exposed to the sky. The pavements are made up of 'grykes' and 'clints', the first being the deep grooves, a haven for lime-loving flowers and ferns as they are out of reach of sheep, the second the blocks of limestone. Streams flowing down from the gritstone that caps the hills disappear into the limestone at sinks or potholes, often re-emerging many kilometres away where the limestone gives way to impervious sandstone. These potholes are the entrance to a vast underground world of caves and passages that make this a major caving area. For the walker they are interesting features to look into and, in my case, shudder.

Of the two pots passed on the descent of Pen-y-ghent, Hunt Pot is a narrow black slash in the hillside, often described as sinister, with a stream running into it. It is around 60m (200ft) deep and was first descended in 1898 by members of the Yorkshire Ramblers Club. Hull Pot is a much larger opening, 90m (300ft) long and 18m (60ft) wide according to most sources, although one gives 45m (145ft) by 25m (85ft) – I haven't measured it myself. The depth seems to be agreed as 18m (60ft). This pot is dry except in floods, the stream normally sinking below the surface higher up the hillside. The water drained by these potholes and many others on Pen-y-ghent reappears near the Pennine Way just north of Horton, at Brants Gill Head. After heavy rain excess water travels on to emerge at Douk Ghyll Scar, south of Brants Gill Head.

Left: *Hull Pot and Pen-y-ghent.*

INGLEBOROUGH

The undisputed overlord of the limestone country, the most compelling presence

A. Wainwright, *Walks in Limestone Country*

Start/finish:	Clapham and Ingleton
Summits:	Ingleborough 724m (2,375ft), Simon Fell 650m (2,133ft)
Distance:	12km (7½ miles)
Navigation:	Moderate
Terrain:	Easy
Winter:	Moderate
Map:	OS 1:25,000 Outdoor Leisure 2: Yorkshire Dales – Western area

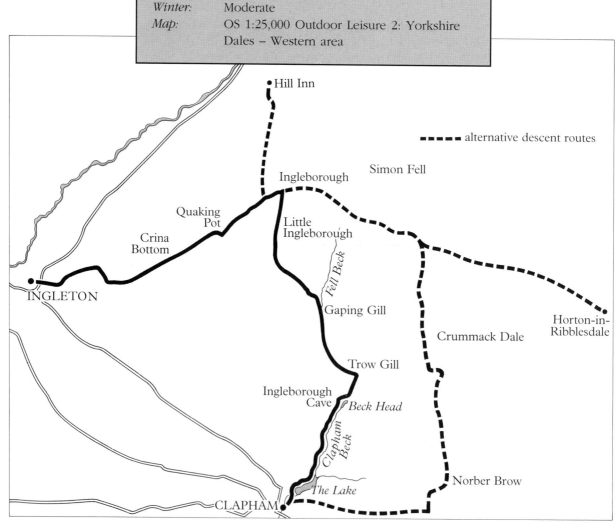

Previous page:
*looking back down
Trow Gill
on the ascent of
Ingleborough from
Clapham.*

Right: *view across
Ribblesdale to
Ingleborough
from the slopes of
Pen-y-ghent.*

On Ingleborough everything the Dales has to offer comes together in a glorious crescendo. This one hill has all the wild variety of limestone scenery on its slopes, plus a fine gritstone summit with superb views. The ascent from Clapham is the best walk in the Dales, probably the best in the Pennines.

Ingleborough is important geologically, botanically and archaeologically, as well as topographically. The third-highest hill in Yorkshire, it was for many years thought to be the highest in England. In part this was probably because of the way it dominates the scenery for miles around, separated as it is by wide valleys from other hills. It can be seen from far away too, the distinctive table-like summit easily identified from many Lake District peaks.

Like other Dales hills, the lower slopes of Ingleborough consist of a band of Great Scar or Mountain limestone some 250m (800ft) thick. The top 305m (1,000ft) is made up of layers of sandstone, limestone and shale topped by a thin layer of gritstone. As elsewhere, water running off the summit disappears into sinks and potholes when it reaches the limestone, emerging again lower down. On Ingleborough, though, there is a greater profusion and variety of limestone features than anywhere else, both above and under the ground. With over 100 sinks and potholes and myriad miles of tunnels and chambers, this is the largest and finest cave area in Britain.

The biggest pothole in Britain, Gaping Gill, is here too. This great chasm is 110m (365ft) deep. Inside it the main chamber, the largest in Britain, is 140m (460ft) long and 30m (100ft) high and wide. After several earlier attempts, the floor was first reached in 1895 by the famous French caver Edouard Martel, who descended on a rope ladder. Today, non-cavers can be winched down in a bosun's chair on summer bank holidays by members of the Bradford and Craven caving clubs. The journey down is free, but you have to pay to come back up!

There are several fine ways to the summit of Ingleborough. Unfortunately, the route taken by the Three Peaks Walk misses most of what is best about the hill, so those who have only climbed it by this route probably wonder why other people are so enthusiastic about it. Far better to make the ascent from the hamlet of Clapham on the southern side of the hill, as near perfect a fell walk as you will find anywhere south of the Highlands. This walk starts beside Clapham Beck, in the rich mixed woodlands of Ingleborough Hall along the Reginald Farrer Nature Trail. Thousands of trees were planted here by the Farrer family last century. In 1833 they constructed the attractive lake passed early in the walk. Reginald Farrer was born in 1880 and became a botanist and plant collector who travelled all over the world in search of new specimens, many of which, such as the Himalayan bamboo, he brought back to plant in the Clapham woods.

As the woods are left behind, the mouth of Ingleborough Cave is passed. Now a popular show cave you can pay to go round, it was first explored in 1837. Clapham Beck issues from the cave having, as Fell Beck, disappeared underground in Gaping Gill. Years of attempts to find the link between the two were finally met with success in 1983.

Above the cave the path enters Trow Gill, a long ravine with walls over 25m (80ft) high, down which the beck that now vanishes into Gaping Gill probably once ran. The floor of this dry valley is rough with boulders and one theory is that it was once a cavern and the boulders the remains of the roof, although there is no real evidence for this. At the end of Trow Gill you exit up a small boulder slope in a narrow slot, probably cut by a waterfall fed by melting glaciers.

Beyond Trow Gill the path heads out on to the open moor and soon passes Gaping Gill, before climbing more steeply to Little Ingleborough and the flat summit of Ingleborough itself.

Here, as well as an OS triangulation column and a large cairn marking the highest point, there is a wind shelter containing a viewfinder, built by the Ingleton Fell Rescue Team in 1953 to commemorate the Coronation of Elizabeth II, which tells you that on a clear day you can see Pendle Hill to the south, Snaefell on the Isle of Man 134km (84 miles) to the west and Scafell in the Lake District to the north, as well as many other hills. I have to say that while I have been on the summit in clear weather several times I have never clearly identified all these summits, but then I have always been more interested in observing nearer hills such as Whernside and Pen-y-ghent than in trying to distinguish distant specks from each other.

The very large cairn where the path from Ingleton reaches the plateau is the remains of a round tower built in 1830. This did not have a long life, as inebriated revellers at the opening ceremony tore down part of it then and there and it was never rebuilt. Older signs of humanity are the outlines of iron-age hut circles that are scattered over the summit and, on the northern and eastern edges, the remains of a wall. This was part of an iron-age hill fort, the largest and highest in the Pennines, that once covered the summit and was probably built by the Brigantes around AD70 as a defence against the Romans. Despite all these features, the plateau can be confusing in mist and careful navigation is required. You need to watch out for others, too. I was up here in thick mist once when I was startled by a sudden loud roaring noise. A second later and two motorcycles rushed out of the mirk and thundered past just a metre or two away. My thoughts on motorbikes in the hills are unprintable!

There are several descent routes from the summit. The best one, however, is – as Wainwright says – the one just ascended from Clapham. If you do not want to retrace your steps you can descend north to the Hill Inn, east to Horton-in-Ribblesdale or west to Ingleton. I would recommend the last, if only because a bus can then be caught back to Clapham. You can also return to Clapham via a rather complicated route that runs over Simon Fell, Ingleborough's subsidiary summit, across the vast limestone pavements of Sulber Scar, down Crummack Dale and past the Norber Boulders, a huge and bizarre collection of erratic boulders transported by a glacier and dumped haphazardly far from their origin.

The path to Ingleton, my favourite of these possible descents, is short, direct, interesting and the easiest in bad weather. It leaves the summit in a south-westerly direction, passes through two small rock bands and then descends open slopes to the small defile of Crina Bottom, where it joins walled Fell Lane. There are several potholes on or near the route, the most interesting being Quaking Pot, a circular hole into which tumbles a thin waterfall. Ingleton itself is a pleasant tourist-orientated village and is the centre for caving in the area.

WILD BOAR FELL AND MALLERSTANG

A great hulk of a hill

Mike Harding, *Walking the Dales*

Start/finish:	Pendragon Castle
Summits:	Wild Boar Fell 708m (2,324ft), Swarth Fell 681m (2,231ft)
Distance:	18km (11 miles)
Navigation:	Difficult
Terrain:	Moderate
Winter:	Moderate
Map:	Harveys 1:25,000 Superwalker: Howgill Fells

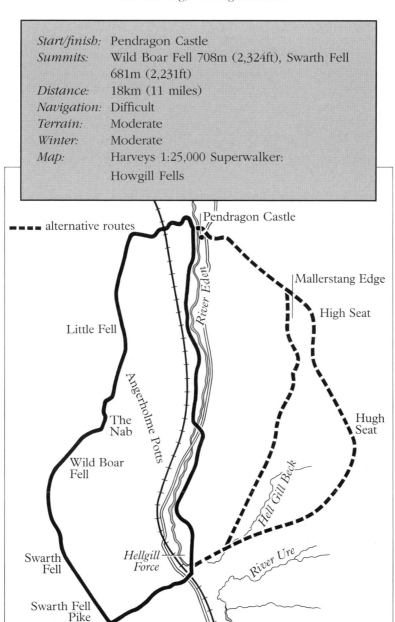

- - - - alternative routes

Pendragon Castle

Mallerstang Edge

High Seat

River Eden

Little Fell

Angerholme Potts

The Nab

Wild Boar Fell

Hugh Seat

Hell Gill Beck

Swarth Fell

Hellgill Force

River Ure

Swarth Fell Pike

'How about Wild Boar Fell, that's about halfway?' It was mid-January and I was arranging a day out on the hills with a friend. However, as he lived in Manchester and I, at the time, on Tyneside, and we did not want to waste any of the few hours of winter daylight, somewhere between the two was required. On consulting the maps, Wild Boar Fell caught my eye. It was a hill I had been intending to climb since walking through the area on an organized event in defence of the Settle–Carlisle railway. Although an excellent walk, that had been a low-level one. Throughout the walk the distinctive bulk of Wild Boar Fell rose tantalizingly above, ensuring I would return there.

We met on a wild, wet morning below the ruins of Pendragon Castle in the upper Eden Valley. Legend says the castle was the birthplace of Uther Pendragon, father of King Arthur, but it is not that old, having been built in the twelfth century as a defence against raids by the Scots, this area being near the Border. The Scots did indeed come, burning the castle in 1340 and again in 1541. In 1660 it was renovated by Lady Anne Clifford, of whom more anon, but since then it has fallen into a picturesque ruin.

The massive bulk of Wild Boar Fell with its sharp eastern escarpment looks dramatic from the castle, dominating the valley. The climb starts by heading west across the railway line before turning

Hell Gill Force in the upper Eden Valley.

south across open moorland to Little Fell. From this minor top the route goes up the steep scarp slopes that make Wild Boar Fell so distinctive from afar, to The Nab on the edge of the summit plateau.

The remains of a bronze-age memorial mound lie on The Nab, but in clear weather it is the views that make this top memorable. Across the valley to the east the 5km (3ml) long line of crags that make up Mallerstang Edge (the unusual name apparently comes from Mallard Stang, meaning Pool of the Mallard) stands out, while in the other direction lie the steep-sided Howgill Fells. Further north and west the flat ridge of High Street in the Lake District can be seen.

Directly north the hills disappear as the wide Vale of Eden spreads out, but to the north-east the land soon rises up again to the summits of the Northern Pennines, with Cross Fell the highest point. On the slopes below The Nab to the east can be seen a line of potholes known as the Angerholme Pots, that mark the break between Wild Boar Fell's gritstone cap and the limestone below.

A short walk across the flat, grassy plateau leads to the summit proper, a trig point inside a circular stone enclosure. The name of the fell reflects the story that the last wild boar in England was killed here in the fifteenth century by Sir Richard Musgrave. The same claim is made for several other places, however. Continuing south, there is a descent to a small tarn and then an easy ascent to Swarth Fell and its southern top, Swarth Fell Pike. From here rough hillside can be descended north-east to the head of the Eden Valley, where you cross the railway by a sign reading 'Aisgill Summit, 1,169ft'. This is the highest point on the Settle–Carlisle railway and

is also on the watershed of England, with the river Ure to the south flowing to the North Sea and the Eden to the north to the Irish Sea.

Once down, you could climb back up the other side and either traverse the summits of Hugh Seat and High Seat before descending to Pendragon Castle, or walk along Mallerstang Edge itself – 'one of the most impressive I have ever done', according to Mike Harding in his excellent book *Walking the Dales*.

Three major northern Pennine rivers – the Ure, the Eden and the Swale – rise on Hugh Seat, which is named after Sir Hugh de Morville of Pendragon Castle, one of the four knights who murdered St Thomas à Becket in Canterbury Cathedral in 1170. The word 'seat' comes from the Norse 'saeter', which means a summer pasture.

On my January walk, time and weather – a thick mist enveloped the tops and light drizzle was beginning to fall – kept us to the low-level walk along valley footpaths back to Pendragon Castle. This is an interesting walk in itself, especially at the southern end where a short climb up to the east leads past the fine 12m (40ft) waterfall of Hell Gill Force to the amazingly deep, narrow gorge of Hell Gill and the wide green track known as the High Way or Lady Anne Clifford's Way, which can be followed back to Pendragon Castle.

Lady Anne Clifford owned many estates from Appleby to Skipton, where she was born in the castle in 1590, and renovated several of the castles on her land including Pendragon. The High Way originally linked Pendragon with her castle in Skipton.

Strolling back to Pendragon with the high fells above and the roaring, rolling Eden close to hand is a pleasant way to end a day on the hills, especially when the weather is wet and windy.

THE HOWGILLS

The whole area is best left alone in poor weather unless considerable experience in map and compass work has been gained.

Gladys Sellars, *The Yorkshire Dales*

Start/finish:	Cross Keys Hotel, 6.5km (4 miles) north-east of Sedbergh on the A683
Summits:	Great Dummacks 661m (2,168ft), Calders 674m (2,211ft), Bram Rigg Top 672m (2,205ft), The Calf 676m (2,218ft), Busk Howe 622m (2,044ft), Fell Head 642m (2,105ft), Randygill Top 624m (2,051ft) Yarlside 638m (2,095ft)
Distance:	20km (12½ miles)
Navigation:	Difficult
Terrain:	Moderate
Winter:	Moderate
Map:	Harveys 1:25,000 Superwalker: Howgill Fells

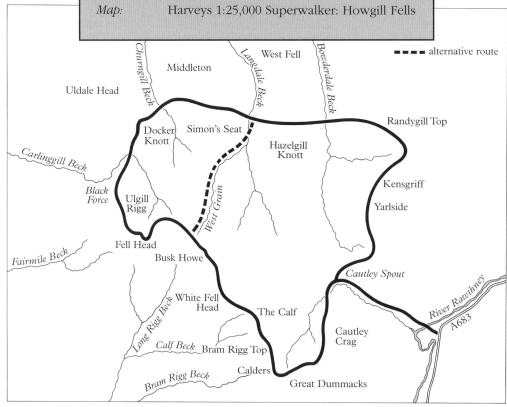

Perched out on their own in the top left-hand corner of the Yorkshire Dales, half in the national park and half out of it, the Howgill Fells are a curious group of isolated hills.

Despite being partly in the Yorkshire Dales park they lie in the county of Cumbria, only a few kilometres from Kendal and the Lake District. Yet they belong to neither the Dales nor the Lakes but stand alone, solitary and independent. Geologically they are made from the same sedimentary rocks (slates, grits and mudstones) as the easternmost fells of the Lakes, and they share with the High Street range the long, grassy ridges and steep-sided valleys such rocks create. Only at Cautley Spout and Black Force are there any cliffs or evidence of glacial action. Elsewhere the hills are smooth-sided and featureless, the rounded summits and long ridges grassy and gently angled. Once up high you can walk for miles over easy terrain.

Even today the Howgills are relatively unknown, probably because of their proximity to the Lakes and the Three Peaks. Many times I stared at their great curving ridges as I travelled up the M6 or the railway to Penrith, vowing to visit them 'one day', before I actually walked on them. A quick study of the map shows that all the tops (there are eight over 610m/2,000ft) could be climbed on one walk, as they all lie on connecting ridges. These form a Y with a truncated tail with the centre being, appropriately, the highest peak, The Calf. You can visit all the tops by going back and forth along the ridges or else by cutting across the intervening valleys, a shorter and more interesting but steeper and rougher route. The summits themselves are rounded and unmemorable: it is the high-level walking that makes the Howgills special.

The narrow, cascading thread of water called Cautley Spout and the splintered rocks of Cautley Crag on the east side of the range are the most popular destinations in the Howgills, and a good footpath leads from the Cross Keys Hotel west across the River Rawthey and up beside the beck to the falls. From here the circuit of the tops can be done in either direction. I prefer clockwise, starting with indistinct and heather-clad Great Dummacks, which lies south of the falls and can be reached by the grassy ridge along the top of Cautley Crag from which you can look down into the depths, although when I first came here all we saw was cloud billowing up from below. There is no path but, as elsewhere in the Howgills, the walking is easy so this is not a problem.

Langdale in the Howgill Fells.

Less than a kilometre west-south-west of Great Dummacks lies the slightly higher Calders from which, on my first visit to these hills, the views were sharp, clear and spacious. To the south and east lay the distinctive outlines of the Three Peaks, west the snow-tinged Lakeland fells, north the dour-looking northern Pennines. Closer to hand to the east, Wild Boar and Baugh Fells rose bulkily across the Rawthey and Sally Beck valleys. Such views can be seen from much of the Howgills, both tops and ridges being fine viewpoints for taking in the wide vistas of England's hill country.

Along the west side of the Howgills lie the deep, steep-sided valleys of Bram Rigg Beck, Calf Beck, Long Rigg Beck and Fairmile Beck, whose intervening ridges make up the most well-known aspect of the Howgills – that seen by countless travellers along the M6 motorway or the main railway line that run at the foot of these spurs. From Calders the route runs northwards above these valleys for several kilometres.

Not far from Calders Bram Rigg Top is reached, and soon afterwards The Calf and then White Fell Head, with a view across the deep valley of Long Rigg Beck to the westernmost Howgill summit Fell Head, itself soon reached with Busk Howe crossed *en route*. This is all easy walking on grassy, gently undulating ground.

From Fell Head a diversion can be made to visit Black Force and the shattered slopes of the upper ravine of Carlinggill Beck. To do this, descend north down Ulgill Rigg to Blakethwaite Bottom, a flat grassy area lying at a height of 400m (1,310ft) between the tops of Uldale Head and Docker Knott on the watershed between Uldale Beck and Carlinggill Beck. This is a superb wild campsite nestling between steep slopes and totally cut off from any sign of civilization. One December I spent a frosty night camping here, waking to a temperature of -2°C (28°F) and a shroud of thick white mist. As the weak winter sun rose, the mists began to dissolve and evaporate to reveal white-frosted slopes and an unreal ghostly hillscape that hovered in the air above the fog-filled valleys.

A little way down Carlinggill Beck lies Black Force. It and the ravine above are grimly impressive, but approaching them requires care due to the steep slopes and loose rocks, a total contrast to the easy terrain of the ridges above.

At Fell Head a decision has to be made. The last two summits, Randygill Top and Yarlside, lie far to the east. Reaching them means either returning along the ridges to The Calf or taking a

direct route across the intervening valleys. I would recommend the latter as more interesting and challenging, although if the mist is down retracing your steps might be wise.

There are two options for the direct route, dependent on whether Black Force is visited. If it is not, the route can be retraced to the col between Fell Head and Busk Howe. From the col the stream of West Grain descends to the north and can be followed to its junction with Langdale Beck. The ridge between Hazelgill Knott and West Fell has to be crossed next, then a descent made to Bowderdale, above which lies Randygill Top.

Visiting Black Force means crossing the ridges of Docker Knott and Simon's Seat–Middleton and the intervening

valley of Churngill Beck before joining the route above in Langdale. The slopes are steep and can be slippery when wet or frosty, but the joy of this route lies in the austere beauty of the three remote valleys, each with a wildness rare in the Pennines.

Randygill Top means a return to the easy walking of the ridges. The last high top, Yarlside, is a short stroll to the south over the minor top of Kensgriff. On my first visit the slopes of Yarlside looked very steep as they rose, still cold and frosty, into the drifting cloud, but the top came soon enough and the short climb was enlivened by an encounter with two of the fell ponies that roam these hills. South of Yarlside lies Cautley Spout and the path back to the start.

The Howgill Fells are typified by grassy hills and deep valleys.

ACROSS THE NORTHERN PENNINES

HIGH CUP AND CROSS FELL

Cross Fell is a surly beast, often in a black mood.
A. Wainwright, *Pennine Way Companion*

Start/finish:	Langdon Beck, Garrigill
Summits:	Cross Fell 893m (2,930ft), Great Dun Fell 848m (2,780ft), Little Dun Fell 842m (2,761ft), Knock Fell 794m (2,604ft)
Distance:	35km (22 miles)
Navigation:	Difficult
Terrain:	Difficult
Winter:	Moderate
Maps:	OS 1:25,000 Outdoor Leisure 31: North Pennines

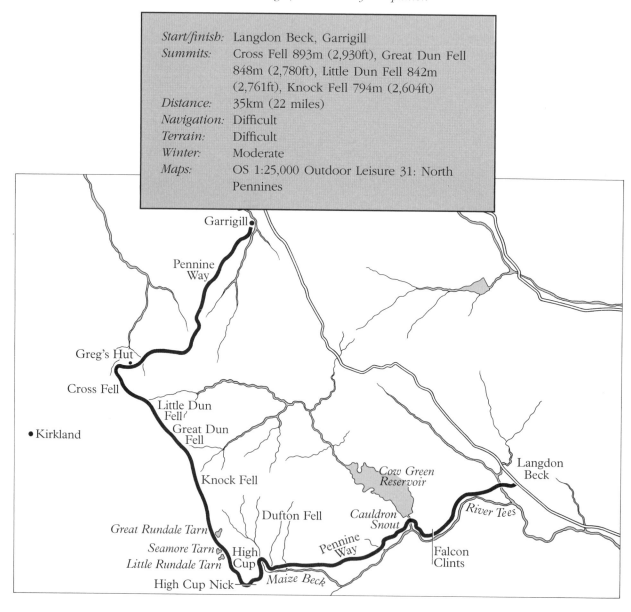

The Northern Pennines are mostly a bleak, wild area of rolling, boggy, curlew-haunted moors where you can walk for days without seeing anyone. These are probably the loneliest hills in England, with far more of a wilderness feel than more frequented areas. Among these featureless uplands lies the highest hill in the Pennines, Cross Fell, and one of the most dramatic sights, High Cup. The Pennine Way links the two, making this one of the few popular walks in the region. It does not make it easy, though, as the terrain is rough and boggy and navigation can be difficult in mist. There is little shelter in bad weather and much of the route lies over 610m (2,000ft).

I first came this way when I first walked the Pennine Way in April 1976, and I can still remember being impressed with the wild feel of the area. Cross Fell was snow-covered and mist-shrouded and felt high and remote. On further visits I have watched the sunset from the summit and bivvied out on its slopes. I have climbed the fell from several directions, but I think the route from the south, mostly along the Pennine Way, is the most interesting and enjoyable. The shortest way to do this is from the attractive village of Dufton to the west, but a better route starts at Langdon Beck youth hostel, as this includes a visit to the defile of High Cup as well as taking in the fine scenery along the upper River Tees.

Although the geology of the Northern Pennines is similar to that to the south, with limestone underlying gritstone, there is one major difference and that is the intrusion of the hard, erosion-resistant igneous rock dolerite, known as the Whin Sill. Forced up as molten lava through the other rocks, dolerite forms dark, columnar outcrops that are far more regular than those of millstone grit.

The first sign of the Whin Sill comes soon after the start of the walk, which runs west from Langdon Beck, in the form of a long, dark cliff on the south side of the wide River Tees. More dolerite rises above the path as it passes along a rocky shelf. This scar is known as Falcon Clints and leads round to the 60m (200ft) torrent of Cauldron Snout, where the Tees cascades down a series of dolerite steps – an impressive sight. The path climbs up beside the water, and as it does so the scene is slowly ruined by the gradual appearance of the dismal, out-of-place, artificial eyesore of Cow Green dam and behind it the grey waters of the reservoir. This was built in the late 1960s despite a campaign by conservationists and the fact that the area was in the Upper Teesdale Nature Reserve because of the unique mountain flora.

Once past this piece of industrial degradation the Pennine Way heads south-west to follow Maize Beck, a major tributary of the Tees, to a ford. This is safe most of the time, but if in doubt a footbridge lies a little way upstream. I can remember hesitating here on one visit when the water was a little higher and faster than usual. As I paused on the brink, two walkers arrived and attempted to cross by jumping from wet rock to wet rock. The first one made it to a couple of rocks, then misjudged the distance to the next one, skidded on the edge and hit the water with a loud splash. He emerged soaked but unhurt and floundered to the bank. I headed for the bridge.

Whichever way you cross Maize Beck, just beyond it is one of the most unexpected and spectacular sights in the Pennines: the perfect U-shaped valley of High Cup. The drab moor suddenly disappears at your feet and drops 200m (600ft) to the floor of the 2½km (1½ miles) long cliff-rimmed rent in the hills – a

surprise view indeed. Even after several
visits, the scene is a shock and a thrill.
That is why it is best to come this way:
approaches from the west give away the
secret gradually and spoil the revelation.

High Cup was formed by a glacier
that tore a great gash in the side of the
Pennines here. The crags along the top
edge are Whin Sill again, and the name
High Cup Nick, often used for the
whole valley, applies to a cleft in these
cliffs at their eastern end. It is worth
approaching the edge of the cliffs,
carefully of course, for a better view of
several detached pinnacles and to gaze
into the depths below.

The Pennine Way descends from
High Cup to the village of Dufton in the
Vale of Eden. Now, while Dufton is a
picturesque village with a pleasant
green, attractive red sandstone houses
and a good pub called The Stag,
descending to it means climbing all the
way back up, so if Cross Fell is the goal
it is better to head north from High Cup
across the pathless moorland of Dufton
Fell, past Little Rundale, Seamore and
Great Rundale Tarns, to rejoin the
Pennine Way after some 4km (2½ miles)
on Knock Fell. Ahead lie Great Dun Fell
and Cross Fell, with rolling waves of
moor rising up to their flat summits.
Unfortunately, the wild scene is spoilt
by the white dome and masts of the
radar station on Great Dun Fell, an
abomination on a mountaintop. If you
want to return to Langdon Beck rather
than finish at Garrigill, you can drop
down east anywhere from the High Cup
to Cross Fell traverse, ford the Tees and
then make your way above Cow Green
Reservoir to the road.

Throughout the walk to Cross Fell
there is a superb view, if the weather is
clear, of the rugged peaks of the Lake
District fells to the west. The walking
itself is somewhat boggy in places,
although much work has been done on

High Cup.

Walkers on the northern slopes of Cross Fell at sunset.

one of the worst sections to the north of the minor top of Little Dun Fell, where a path of stone flags has been laid. These are starkly noticeable at present, but should weather into the surroundings with time and allow the wide eroded tracks to either side to recover from the pressure of too many boots.

Finally, the slopes of Cross Fell itself are reached and the ground steepens briefly for the final pull up through the rocks that rim the extensive, grassy summit plateau. Despite various cairns, a trig point and a large cross-shaped wind shelter, it is easy to get confused here in mist and a close eye should be kept on the compass. Snow lies long here too, sometimes into July, and may prove a problem in the winter when it can be quite deep.

The original name for Cross Fell was Fiend's Fell. A legend says that the name was changed after St Augustine built a cross on the summit and drove away the devils that lived there. However, the hill was still referred to as Fiend's Fell long after St Augustine's time. There is a Fiend's Fell not far to the north-west, so perhaps the name was changed to avoid confusion with this top (or perhaps this is where the devils went!)

As with other flat-topped Pennine hills, Cross Fell was used for various events during the last century, the biggest one probably being in 1832 when 50 brass bands played on the summit to celebrate the passing of the Reform Act.

Cross Fell is also famous for the Helm Wind, the only named local wind in Britain. The wind appears when east or north-east winds hit the peak, roll over the top and then pick up speed as they roar down the steep western slopes. Signs of the wind are the appearance of a cloud cap over the summit, known as the Helm, and a long band of cloud some 8km (5mls) to the west, called the Helm Bar. Very strong winds often sweep the exposed summit plateau, making the wind shelter very welcome, but these are not the Helm Wind, which only occurs low down on the western slopes.

The route now drops down the rough northern flanks of Cross Fell to turn eastwards along a track known as the Corpse Road, over which coffins were carried from Garrigill village – where there was no graveyard – to Kirkland to the west. Shortly after this track is reached spoil heaps from old mines appear, and then a small bothy known as Greg's Hut. This old miner's cottage was restored by the Mountain Bothies Association in 1972 in memory of one John Gregory of the Mercian Mountaineering Club, killed while ski touring in the Alps. In summer this is a popular place for Pennine Wayfarers to overnight. I did so twice in the late 1970s and had the place to myself each time, but that was in the months of April and May. If the bothy is full there are plenty of good campsites nearby. Indeed, on my last visit, on a trip organized for outdoor writers by the equipment manufacturers Mountain Range who are based in nearby Alston, I bivvied out near the bothy with 17 others. Despite the proximity of all those other people, I still found myself a sheltered spot below a low bank where I was and felt alone, and where I could lie quietly in my sleeping bag as

the last of the red sunset faded from the sky and the first stars appeared and the pale moon rose. I felt even more solitary on waking to a thick, damp mist the next morning as the bothy, less than a hundred metres away, was no more than a faint blur and my companions invisible.

Cross Fell and the surrounding moors are riddled with shafts and levels, mostly cut for lead, although silver was mined here too, and there are extensive remains of this industry around Greg's Hut. There is evidence that the Romans mined lead here and it may be that the Celts did so even earlier. Mining continued from Roman times, but the maximum output was between 1700 and 1900. It is hard to imagine trying to make a living digging ore high on the slopes of these cold, wet hills. It must have been a tough life. While the spoil heaps can be explored, I would stay out of any underground workings as many are highly dangerous. Take care too not to fall into hidden shafts. Relics should not be damaged either: they are historic artefacts that have already decayed a great deal. If you want to learn more about this important industry, the Heritage Centres at Killhope Wheel and Nenthead are worth visiting.

From Greg's Hut the Pennine Way descends gradually to Garrigill on a wide track with good views of the South Tyne Valley. Garrigill offers a store, a café and a pub, but if you need public transport you will have to go on another 5km (3mls) to Alston, the highest market town in England with fine cobbled streets and interesting old buildings, where buses run to the railway station at Haltwhistle. Langdon Beck lies about 16km (10 miles) to the south of Garrigill on the B6277.

FOUR

THE LAKE
DISTRICT

BEAUTIFUL lakes, verdant woodlands, crashing water-falls, high coombes, sparkling tarns, great cliffs, pinnacled aretes, long grassy ridges, rugged rocky mountain summits: there is so much packed into the small corner of north-west England called the Lake District that it is hardly a surprise that this is many walkers' favourite area. It is also perhaps where hillwalking as a leisure pursuit started with the wanderings of Romantic poets Wordsworth and Coleridge, as well as being the birthplace of rock climbing with W. Haskett-Smith's 1886 ascent of Napes Needle, a rock spire on the slopes of Great Gable.

Today the 2,280sq km (880sq miles) Lake District National Park is extremely popular and can seem grossly overcrowded on holiday weekends. However, most people do not wander far from their cars and those who do venture into the hills tend to stick to the most popular ones – Helvellyn, Scafell Pike, Great Gable – and the most popular paths. It is still possible to find solitude here, even on a bank holiday.

Partly this is because of the number of hills – 170 over 610m (2,000ft), although only four are above 914m (3,000ft). The Lake District hills are not a single unit of course, and there are significant differences between the various groups. In the north and north-west the fells are big, rounded whalebacks and there are few cliffs. This is because the underlying rock is a type of slate, called Skiddaw slate from the highest mountain in the area, that shatters easily into small fragments and so does not readily form crags. The rest of the fells are mainly made from the hard, rough rocks known as Borrowdale volcanics. West of the A591 road from Ambleside to Keswick the fells are rugged and rocky with a complex topography. East of the road the scenery is somewhat simpler, centred around two long south–north running ridges. Although there are still cliffs, the fells are generally gentler. Wherever you go in the Lakes, though, the walking is superb.

THE LANGDALE HORSESHOE

CRINKLE CRAGS, BOWFELL AND THE LANGDALE PIKES

One of the finest and most varied fell walks in the district.

Tom Price, *The Big Walks*

Start/finish:	Elterwater
Summits:	Lingmoor Fell 470m (1,541ft), Side Pike 362m (1,187ft), Cold Pike 701m (2,300ft), Pike O'Blisco 705m (2,313ft), Crinkle Crags 859m (2,818ft), Bowfell 902m (2,959ft), Rossett Pike 651m (2,136ft), Pike O'Stickle 709m (2,362ft), Harrison Stickle 736m (2,415ft), Pavey Ark 700m (2,297ft), Blea Rigg 556m (1,823ft), Silver Howe 393m (1,292ft)
Distance:	30km (18 miles)
Navigation:	Moderate
Terrain:	Moderate
Winter:	Difficult
Map:	Harveys 1:25,000 Superwalker: Western Lakeland. OS 1:25,000 Outdoor Leisure 6: The English Lakes – South-Western area

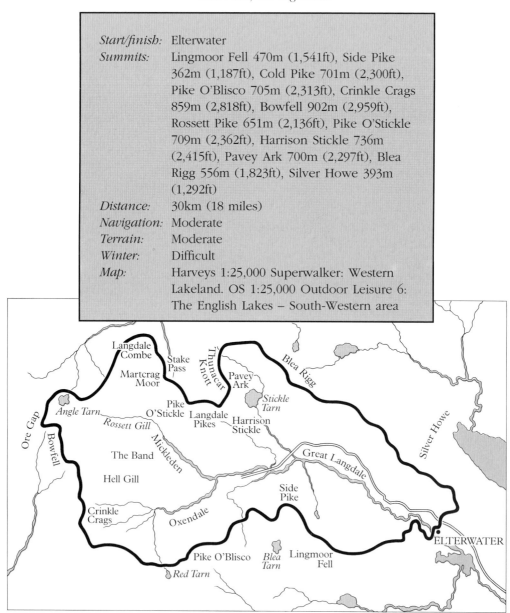

Great Langdale is one of the most beautiful and most popular valleys in the Lake District. Walled by fine peaks, it is a mountain valley *par excellence*. The most well-known fells are the Langdale Pikes, whose outline is instantly identifiable and has appeared in innumerable pictures of the Lake District. The walking possibilities in and around Langdale are many, but my favourite walk is the round of all the tops, the Langdale Horseshoe. The short version of this begins at the famous Old Dungeon Ghyll hotel and takes in the highest tops only. The full walk, however, starts at Elterwater at the foot of the valley. Although a long route there are many easy ways back down into the valley, so it can be abandoned at any time for any reason, whether the advent of bad weather or darkness, exhaustion or simply being unable to overcome the desire for a pint in one of the hotels below.

There are good reasons for doing the walk both clockwise and anti-clockwise. The solution of course is to do it twice (at least!). However, for the first-timer I would recommend clock-wise, if only because of the superb and complete view of the whole route to be had from the first summit, Lingmoor Fell. This is reached by a rather complicated route, wooded for the first half, that starts by heading north-west out of Elterwater on the path beside Great Langdale Beck. After a short distance the path leaves the beck to climb south-west through Sawrey's Wood and the old quarry workings, before emerging on to the open fellside and continuing on to the summit.

On the summit, a scenic split evident throughout the walk appears. Ahead and to either side rise rugged fells, subtly coloured and with an austere mien. Behind, to the east, lies opulence and ease as richly wooded, brightly

green lowlands spread out around shining pools towards the long dark strip of Windermere.

We are heading for the heights, and so turn our backs on the luxury below and head north-west for little rocky Side Pike, which hangs right on the edge of the valley directly opposite the Langdale Pikes and the crag-strewn hillside below them. A short drop to the Blea Tarn road and the ascent of the first of the high tops, Pike O'Blisco, is begun. Although rough and rocky, this is an easier hill to climb than it looks, something true of many of the Langdale fells. The summit is tiny and rocky, a true mountain peak.

Scrambling in Hell Gill on the ascent of Bowfell from Oxendale.

Previous pages: Descending into Upper Eskdale from Esk Hause.

85

The next fell, Cold Pike, can be skirted on its north side, but it is a good viewpoint and worth the extra effort. Beyond Cold Pike flatter terrain leads north-eastwards towards Crinkle Crags, a long undulating ribbon of small rocky knobs rather than a single fell. The traverse of this ridge is enjoyable and entertaining throughout and only at one avoidable spot at all difficult or exposed. This last occurs just south of the highest point and is a short, steep rock wall known as the Bad Step. It is only about 3m (10ft) high and has a couple of good well-worn holds, but it can still cause problems, especially in descent. The alternative is a path to the west that rounds the base of all the rocks on the south side of the summit.

After Crinkle Crags comes one of my

Harrison Stickle and Stickle Gill.

favourite Lakeland hills, Bowfell. The view of this magnificent peak as you descend to Three Tarns is superb, with the rough seamed and ridged south face, called Bowfell Links, apparently barring the way to the top. Three Tarns, around which there are many sheltered campsites that I have used on several occasions, is a major crossroads with paths descending into Upper Eskdale

and Great Langdale. Our path goes up the broad, stony south-east buttress to the right of Bowfell Links and then curves west over the chaotic summit boulder field to the top. Below to the east lie some impressive crags that can be visited on an alternative route, which descends a short way from Three Tarns down the spur known as The Band (the most popular way up Bowfell) and then takes the Climber's Traverse below Flat Crags, the Great Slab and Cambridge Crags. Beyond the last there is a break in the rock wall where a wide scree gully leads upwards. This is the walker's way through the cliffs. Go on a little way, though, to the foot of Bowfell Buttress, a spectacular piece of rock up which runs a relatively easy but highly impressive rock climb, the eponymous Bowfell Buttress (graded Very Difficult which, in rock-climbing language, means not at all difficult). The valley below is Mickleden (from the Old English 'micel denu' or 'great valley').

On the other, southern, side of The Band, which splits the head of Great Langdale in two, is Oxendale, which contains a number of easy scrambling lines that are far better than The Band as a route from the valley to Three Tarns and Crinkle Crags or Bowfell. My favourite, perhaps because of memories of climbing it on an idyllic hot, sunny day when the spray of the cool water was a welcome relief, is Hell Gill, a short but pleasant scramble.

The descent from Bowfell leads down rough, stony slopes to Ore Gap, named for the haematite – iron ore – that stains the soil red here. From this pass a steep path leads north above the deep bowl containing Angle Tarn, a dramatic spot. The route now heads south-east as it crosses the head of Rossett Gill, the most popular way on to the fells from Mickleden, before climbing a gentle grassy slope to Rossett

Pike, a rocky top that looks very impressive from the lower slopes of Rossett Gill.

Heading north again to avoid the drop into Langdale Combe we descend to boggy Stake Pass, an old packhorse route between Langdale and Borrowdale, where the route turns south-east. Damp, soft ground continues as Martcrag Moor is crossed. This is perhaps the dullest walking on the route but not far ahead are the Langdale Pikes, a good reason to keep going. First comes the rocky cone of Pike O'Stickle. An easy scramble leads to the neat summit, from which there is a stupendous view down steep slopes into Mickleden. The scree-covered hillside just below the summit is the site of a neolithic stone axe factory, and axes from this site have been found all over Europe.

Although only short distances separate the tops making up the Langdale Pikes and there are many well-worn paths, it is still possible to lose your way in mist, especially if you do not have a map or compass! The only time I have been here without such essential items was on a walk organized by a well-known outdoor-equipment manufacturer as a promotion for a new rucksack. The list of gear we were asked to bring did not include map or compass and as this was a guided walk, foolishly, I did not carry them. Unfortunately neither did anyone else, including the guides, as we found when, having split into two parties, we met up in thick mist somewhere between Harrison Stickle and Pike O'Stickle. Without actually asking and therefore having to admit that they were confused as to where they were, each

group tried to find out from the other the way to proceed. A bit of guesswork, most of us having walked here many times before, solved the problem, but it could have been embarrassing. Imagine the headlines if the rescue team had been called out to find a party of outdoor writers, outdoor-gear company staff and professional guides. I have never gone on any trip, however well organized, without a map and compass since, and I believe that everybody in a party should carry them and know how to use them.

Back down on the moor from Pike O'Stickle good paths lead to the last two high tops, Harrison Stickle and Pavey Ark, which give great views to the valley below and down to Stickle Tarn. I have to say, though, that as it is the southern faces of these tops that are the most impressive, their north sides fading away into the moorland of Thunacar Knott (probably the dullest summit in the Lakes), the approaches from Great Langdale are the best, with the ascent of the great cliff of Pavey Ark by way of Jack's Rake – an easy, if long and in places exposed scramble – being the finest of all.

The walk now slowly and pleasantly leaves the high mountains, rounding the head of Bright Beck just north of Pavey Ark and then wandering south-east-wards down the long ridge of Blea Rigg to the final top, beautiful, grassy and surprisingly complex Silver Howe, from where there is a good view of Grasmere. Elterwater lies just to the south and can be reached by descending the path down the south-east ridge of Silver Howe, until it crosses a path heading south that leads directly to the village.

WALK

14

THE SCAFELLS

*I ascended Sca'Fell by the side of a torrent, and climbed
and rested, rested and climbed, 'till I gained the very
summit of Sca'Fell.*

Samuel Taylor Coleridge, *Collected Letters*

Start/finish:	Seathwaite, Borrowdale
Summits:	Great End 910m (2,986ft), Ill Crag 935m (3,068ft), Broad Crag 934m (3,064ft), Scafell Pike 978m (3,209ft), Scafell 964m (3,163ft)
Distance:	14km (9 miles)
Navigation:	Difficult
Terrain:	Difficult
Winter:	Very difficult
Map:	Harveys 1:25,000 Superwalker: Western Lakeland. OS: 1:25,000 Outdoor Leisure 6: The English Lakes – South-Western area

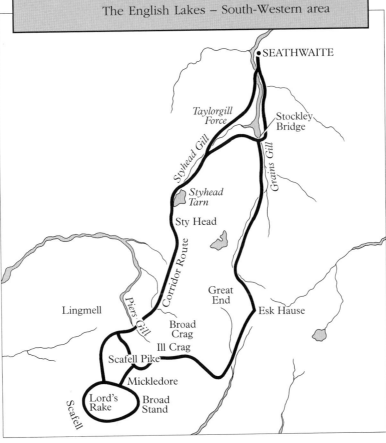

I first climbed Scafell Pike as a school-boy, slogging up Rossett Gill from Langdale on a very hot, windless day and then floundering over what seemed never-ending stones and boulders to the summit. The final dip and ascent beyond Broad Crag was almost too much for a thirsty, tired 13-year-old who had never been anywhere like this before, but I kept on, although now I have no recollection of reaching the summit. I have been back many times to climb both Scafells from every direction, often camping out on their flanks; I have scrambled up their rocky sides and run over them on mountain marathons – and every time I go back I am surprised at just how good they are, at just how wild, rugged, impressive and challenging this, the highest land in England, is.

Scafell and Scafell Pike are the highest points on a ridge that separates Wasdale and Upper Eskdale, a ridge of broken, shattered rocks buttressed by massive cliffs and spurs. The slopes everywhere are steep and there is little flat ground, even on the ridge top. Deep ravines carry water down the mountainsides and the few tarns are tiny and hemmed in with crags. Even the easiest walking routes involve crossing large areas of boulders and stones. As Wainwright says, 'sufferers from bad feet must expect an orgy of torture on any of these ascents'.

The peaks can be climbed most directly from Wasdale, and by longer approaches from Great Langdale and Borrowdale. All the routes from these valleys to Scafell Pike are very popular, the rough nature of the terrain not enough to stop people wanting to stand on the highest mountain in England. Scafell is less popular, in part I suspect because linking it with Scafell Pike is quite difficult.

The least-visited, remotest side of the Scafells is that above Upper Eskdale, a wild, beautiful valley, and it is here, in my opinion, that the best ascents are to be found. The obvious way to Upper

Autumn mists in the woods of Borrowdale.

Eskdale is from lower Eskdale, but it is actually hardly any further from Seathwaite at the head of Borrowdale, which is much more accessible than Eskdale.

The walk begins with the good path south from Seathwaite to Stockley Bridge, and then up beside Grains and Ruddy Gill to the major walkers' crossroads of Esk Hause. The high point of this approach is the sight of the massive cliff of Great End, which dominates the view. This is the end of the Scafell ridge and can be climbed easily from Esk Hause, with the stony ridge then followed to Scafell Pike. There are good scrambling routes up the face of Great End, with Central Gully perhaps the best for confident scramblers.

In winter the terrain hereabouts can be confusing, as I know from a visit many years ago when I climbed Great End by mistake. Two of us set off from Seathwaite on a grey late-November day with all the tops in mist. Deep snow covered all landmarks and filled the stream gullies. Not concentrating, we got our timings completely wrong, thinking, unusually, that we were going much slower than we were. Unsure of our whereabouts, as they say, but feeling we must be around Esk Hause, we cut towards where we thought the base of the Great End cliffs should be. We found some steep slopes sure enough, but they were below us and we seemed to be on a top. Totally perplexed by now, we retraced our steps. Encountering another party, we chose safety over pride and asked them where we were. Descending Great End, came the reply. I cannot imagine what they said as we wandered off, completely baffled, but it probably wasn't complimentary.

But back to Esk Hause and Upper Eskdale. The view from Esk Hause (the upper or true Esk Hause that is) down Eskdale to the Scafells is magnificent. A line of buttresses runs along the side of the peaks, with the neat subsidiary summit of Pen prominent. Descending Upper Eskdale on sketchy paths, you soon come to the south-east face of Ill Crags, a broad buttress covered with slabs, ribs and walls of rock separated by steep slopes and shelves of grass and heather, up which you can scramble. The route can be as easy or as hard as you like to make it. Those keen on rock can climb some quite difficult sections where a rope may be welcome. All these can be avoided, however, and you can walk most of the way. The atmosphere is tremendous and the lack of people, paths and cairns and the emptiness of the unspoilt valley below give it a wilderness feel rare in the Lake District.

The scramble ends on the summit of Ill Crag, from where you can quickly join the main path to Scafell Pike, with the option of making the extremely short but very rocky diversion to the boulders that make up the top of Broad Crag.

The summit of Scafell Pike is marked by a massive cairn. There is also a trig point and a plethora of wind shelters. Otherwise, it is just a bleak jumble of stones. The views when it is clear are far reaching but, as so often from the highest peaks of an area, not that impressive, as everything in view is lower than you are.

A rocky descent leads south-west to Mickledore, the narrow col between Scafell Pike and Scafell. Astride the far end of Mickledore is the huge Scafell Crag, 150m (500ft) high and the biggest in England. There is a route directly up this cliff by way of Broad Stand, but this is only for rock climbers or very competent, confident scramblers. It is the way Coleridge descended from

Early-morning mist clearing over Borrowdale.

Scafell in 1802, an impressive achievement as the route was completely unexplored until then.

Luckily there are two easier alternatives to Broad Stand: Foxes Tarn to the south and Lord's Rake and the West Wall Traverse to the west. The last is best for ascent, leaving the easier Foxes Tarn line for the descent. To reach Lord's Rake, descend the scree next to the crag westwards until a steep scree gully appears above you. This is the rake. It is steep and awkward to climb, especially as much of the scree has gone with the passage of thousands of boots. The rock scenery on either side makes up for the difficulties, however. Near the top of the gully the West Wall Traverse cuts left into the upper part of Deep Gill, a huge cleft that splits the cliffs, leaving a final steep scree scramble to the top of the cliffs. It is a magnificent route that brings the walker into the world of the rock climber in a way that few scrambles can.

The summit of Scafell is now just a short stroll away to the south. After the scramble it is a rather unexciting, tame place without the bleak grandeur of Scafell Pike. To return to Mickledore,

follow a scree path south-east to the tiny pool of Foxes Tarn and then scramble easily down the outlet stream gully to a narrow path, which runs under the vertical East Buttress back up to Mickledore.

From Mickledore you can descend into the top of the great bowl of Hollow Stones, then follow the Climber's Traverse under Pikes Crag to Lingmell col, where the Corridor Route starts its traverse of the rough, steep, chasm-split northern flanks of the Scafell massif. This is an excellent route that takes the only easy way across these slopes. It crosses several ravines including the head of Piers Gill, an impressively deep, sheer-sided gash in the north side of Lingmell, first climbed in 1892. The Corridor Route is popular and in places the path has undergone extensive repair work. It finishes at Styhead, from where the even more popular path beside Styhead Gill can be taken down to Stockley Bridge and Seathwaite. If you still have some energy left, a better route is that on the other side of the gill which descends, at times down steep, narrow slabs of rock, through rock scenery past the waterfall of Taylorgill Force.

GREAT GABLE AND THE CLIMBER'S TRAVERSE

'Great' indeed!

John Wyatt, *The Lake District National Park*

Start/finish:	Honister Pass
Summits:	Great Gable 899m (2,949ft), Green Gable 801m (2,628ft), Brandreth 715m (2,346ft), Grey Knotts 697m (2,287ft)
Distance:	10km (6 miles)
Navigation:	Moderate
Terrain:	Difficult
Winter:	Difficult
Map:	Harveys 1:25,000 Superwalker: Western Lakeland. OS 1:25,000 Outdoor Leisure 4: The English Lakes – North-Western area

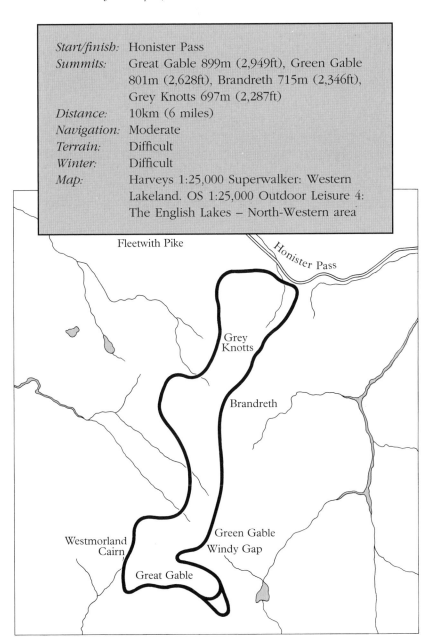

Great Gable is probably the most popular fell in the Lake District. Helvellyn may, just, have more ascents, but it does not claim the affections of walkers in the way that Great Gable does. When I started hillwalking this was the peak everyone wanted to climb and the one people talked about afterwards. Its popularity is in the main due to its striking appearance, making it easily identifiable from afar. The shape changes according to the viewpoint – a pyramid from the south (the house gable end that gives it its name), a flat-topped block from the east and west, a steep-sided dome from the north – but from every direction it is a distinct separate mountain. It rises over 400m (1,300ft) above Styhead to the south-east, 150m (500ft) above the narrow col of Windy Gap to the north-east and 380m (1,250ft) above Beck Head to the north-west. These are the closest points between Great Gable and other fells. There are no easy ridges connecting it to other peaks, nor are there any easy ways up – all are steep and stony. Great Gable is a rock mountain with little vegetation or water on the upper slopes.

Great Gable is best seen from Wasdale. The view of the mountain, framed by its satellites and towering above Wastwater, is the emblem of the national park and it is a striking sight. Great Gable is often climbed from Wasdale too, by way of Beck Head or Styhead, but these routes involve long approaches over steep scree and are not my favourites. Seathwaite and Ennerdale are other possible start points, but my preferred ascent starts at Honister Pass to the north which has the advantage of being at 360m (1,200ft), although this is not the main reason for choosing this route.

The initial environs of Honister are not promising, due to the huge quarry rising above. Three hundred years of slate removal have ripped the hillsides apart. This industrial devastation can very quickly be left behind, however, for the open fellside. The path to take is signposted for Great Gable, Black Sail and Dubs, and starts by heading west

On the Climber's Traverse, Great Gable.

from Honister and climbing to the large flat area east of Fleetwith Pike, where it turns south and heads directly for Great Gable.

This path is called Moses Trod (trod is a local dialect word for path). It is an old pack-horse route once used for transporting slate from the Honister quarries over to Wasdale and then down to the Esk estuary, a total distance of 24km (15 miles). Moses himself is a legendary figure, who is said to have smuggled whisky along the route.

Smugglers route or not, Moses Trod is a marvellous walk. Ingeniously engineered to contour round the fellside with a minimum of climbing, it curves round the slopes of Grey Knotts and Brandreth and the head of Ennerdale to Beck Head. For a traverse it has a surprisingly open feel, almost like being on a ridge. The views of Ennerdale and its surrounding peaks are superb, while in front Great Gable draws the eye. As you approach the peak, the grim dark face of Gable Crag, perpetually in shadow, dominates the scene. There is no way up this cliff for the walker. To the left lies Windy Gap, which we will cross on the descent. The path now turns west and runs below Gable Crag to the pass of Beck Head, between Gable Beck and Tongue Beck, which descend to Wasdale and Ennerdale respectively. Also at Beck Head is the start of the Climber's Traverse.

This route leads across the south face of Great Gable right below the cliffs known as The Napes. Originally a way for rock climbers to reach the start of their climbs, hence the name, it is a superb route for walkers who do not mind a bit of easy scrambling and revel in magnificent rock architecture. More competent scramblers could take some of the easier routes up the cliffs. Initially a contour across steep scree and boulders, the traverse rounds the south-

west ridge, where a path leads down Gavel Neese to Wasdale, then passes below the shattered rocks of the White Napes. The Great Napes is only a little further. Rather than a single huge rock or cliff, this is a collection of rock ridges that come together at their apex, where a short narrow ridge connects them to the main fell. They are edged to either side by long ribbons of steep red-coloured scree called Little Hell Gate and Great Hell Gate. Both lead to the top of The Napes, from where the summit of Gable is easily reached. I do not recommend this, however, having climbed Great Hell Gate on a very hot summer day. The loose scree slid down at every step and progress was arduous and slow. Dust exploded in clouds at every step and stuck to the sweat on my skin, and I reached the top exhausted and dirty. There are easier ways. Much easier ways.

Threading a way through the lower rocks, the traverse passes below the famous Napes Needle, an 18m (60ft) pinnacle first climbed by W. Haskett-Smith in 1886 and generally taken to be the climb that started rock climbing in Britain, although two years earlier he had climbed the ridge above, Needle Ridge. Once across Great Hell Gate the going becomes easier, and the path curves round the fellside to Styhead Pass. A wide, well-used path, known as the Breast Route and renovated in places, heads up the broad south-west slopes of the mountain to the summit, a steep but easy and very popular path. The only time I have been here when it was not crowded was after a night spent by Styhead Tarn, when we were on the summit before most people had had breakfast. The first of the hordes were met on the track down to Wasdale.

The summit of Great Gable is a fine rocky spot. The views are extensive in all directions, the Scafells looking particularly fine. A war memorial, in the form of a plaque provided by the Fell and Rock Club in memory of their members who died in World War I, is set in the summit rocks. A service is held here on Remembrance Sunday.

A classic view of Wasdale can be had by walking some 150m (160yd) south-west of the summit to a large well-made cairn on the edge of steep crags. This is Westmorland Cairn, named for the two brothers who built it in 1876 to mark what they regarded as the finest view in the Lakes. At your feet lie the white-walled green fields of Wasdale, with Wastwater beyond them and the fells rising to either side.

The summit is left by a steep, rocky descent to the north-east that brings you down to Windy Gap, from where the neat summit of Green Gable is but a short stroll. A pleasant high-level walk back to Honister now ensues, taking in the tops of Brandreth and Grey Knotts. In clear weather there are good views throughout. In mist the line of fence posts joined on the south slopes of Brandreth will be welcome. They lead all the way back to Honister Pass.

Great Gable from the south.

GRASMOOR AND THE COLEDALE HORSESHOE

Arguably the best combination of linked ridges in the Lake District.

Walt Unsworth, *Classic Walks in the Lake District*

Start/finish:	Braithwaite
Summits:	Causey Pike 637m (2,090ft), Scar Crags 672m (2,205ft), Sail 773m (2,536ft), Crag Hill 839m (2,753ft), Grasmoor 852m (2,795ft), Hopegill Head 770m (2,525ft), Hobcarton Crag 739m (2,425ft), Grisedale Pike 791m (2,595ft)
Distance:	16km (10 miles)
Navigation:	Moderate
Terrain:	Easy
Winter:	Difficult
Map:	Harveys 1:25,000 Superwalker: North West Lakeland. OS 1:25,000 Outdoor Leisure 4: The English Lakes – North Western area

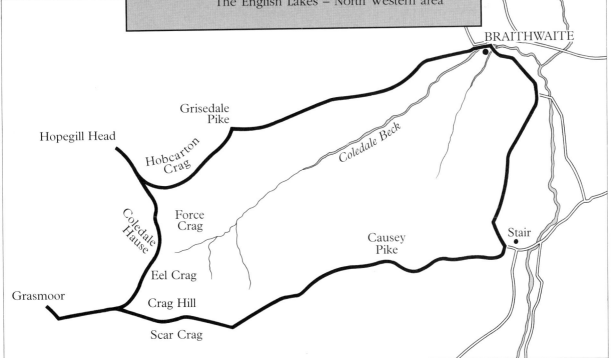

The Lake District fells are generally thought of as rough and rocky. Craggy peaks of rock and stone rising above green valleys and deep lakes typify the region. It is not all like that, though. In the north and north-west the underlying rock is Skiddaw slate rather than Borrowdale volcanic and the fells are grassy and rounded. There are crags, but these rim the heads of valleys or hang well down the sides of the hills, leaving the summits and ridges smooth and even.

In the north-western fells a series of ridges makes for easy high-level walking. The area bounded by Buttermere, the Newlands valley and Whinlatter Pass contains 16 tops that rise above 610m (2,000ft). It is quite possible to visit all of these in one walk, although this would involve a fair bit of repetition.

The centre of this wealth of ridges is grassy Coledale Hause, a surprisingly wide and flat pass linking Braithwaite with Lanthwaite. The best walk in the district revolves around this hub, following the ridges around Coledale, the valley at whose head it lies. There are seven summits on this ridge but most walkers will want to add Grasmoor, the highest fell in the area, as it is not far to the south-west of Coledale Hause. Other summits can be added too. It all depends on how much time and energy you have.

The views throughout the walk are panoramic and excellent, and one of the joys is that the soft ground underfoot and the rounded nature of the ridges mean that you can enjoy the vistas as you walk. Walkers who like to stride out rhythmically and find rocky terrain disturbs their progress will appreciate this.

The village of Braithwaite near Keswick is the best start point for the walk. I prefer to go clockwise, although there is no strong reason for doing so.

The steep ridge leading to Causey Pike, the first peak, starts above the hamlet of Stair in the Newlands Valley, a couple of kilometres easy valley walking from Braithwaite, although the fell can be reached by the path up Barrow Gill. Causey Pike is a very distinctive fell, with a series of little rocky tops making up the summit. Really it is the northern end of the long eastern ridge of Eel Crag and, like the other tops beyond it, a subsidiary top of that peak.

Scar Crags is the next top, soon reached on a good path. The view down the steep southern slopes to Rigg Beck is quite impressive but the top itself is unmemorable, just a rise in the ridge. The next fell, Sail, although higher, is even more forgettable, especially with the sight of the narrow east ridge of Eel Crag ahead. Nowhere is this difficult, however, although there are rocks in places.

The name Eel Crag is more correctly applied to the crags north of the summit, the fell being Crag Hill. This is how the OS gives it anyway, but Harveys have Eel Crag as the name of the fell as a whole and mention Crag Hill not all. Whatever you call it, this is a fine fell and the culmination of the ridge from Causey Pike. Triangular in shape, it has crags on both the northern and southern sides, with the east ridge running up between them.

Eel Crag lies at the head of Coledale and is therefore the turning point of the walk. However, Grasmoor is close by and well worth ascending if the weather is clear. In mist it can be very confusing, as the terrain is quite featureless. To reach Grasmoor, head west. The climb up wide, grassy slopes is gentle: it seemed endless on one hot, still July day when I was undertaking my first two-day mountain marathon. This had begun at Braithwaite but the first checkpoint was on the summit of

A camp on Coledale Hause looking north to Skiddaw and Blencathra.

Grasmoor. Getting there certainly spread everybody out. I arrived on the top soaked in sweat and already partly dehydrated, a condition that was to last the rest of the day. There is little water high in these fells and the litre I had set off with was long gone.

From this side Grasmoor does not look very significant, buttressed as it is by many other fells. To the west, though, it drops abruptly to Crummock Water, from where it is an impressive sight. As well as being the steepest, this side of the fell is also the roughest, with many crags. The summit is large, with a huge cairn and wind shelter. A large coombe has been carved out of the northern edge of the summit and the back of this forms Dove Crags, which can be seen clearly on the descent to Coledale Hause.

Like many Lakeland passes, Coledale Hause is an excellent camping spot in good weather. Waking to the excellent view of Skiddaw and Blencathra to the north is an inspiring way to start the day.

From the Hause, Hopegill Head is quickly ascended over the insignificant bump of Sand Hill. There is further confusion over names here, the fell sometimes being called Hobcarton Pike, after Hobcarton Crags which make up its northern slopes. The OS has Hopegill Head, while Harveys cover themselves with Hopegill Head or Hobcarton Pike. Unlike most of the other felltops in this area the summit is tiny – a real peak.

The shattered rocks of Hobcarton Crags are of no interest to climbers, which is probably a good thing as they are botanically significant, being the only place in England where the red alpine catchfly, *Viscaria alpina*, grows. It is a pretty flower which I have seen many times in the mountains of Scandinavia, where it is common. My guide to Scandinavian mountain flowers says it 'prefers soils rich in pyrites and heavy metals', which may say something about the geology of the crags. There are old mines not far away in Coledale, one of which, Force Crag Mine, is still worked intermittently for barytes.

The edge of the crags can be followed on the way to the narrow slate-covered top of Grisedale Pike, last on the round. This is a well-known peak, as its distinctive summit can be seen clearly from Keswick. From here you can look back to all the summits, including Grasmoor, before descending easily down the north-east ridge to Braithwaite.

THE OTHER FAIRFIELD HORSESHOE

A grand mountain with grand satellites in support.

A. Wainwright, *The Eastern Fells*

Start/finish:	Patterdale
Summits:	St Sunday Crag 841m (2,759ft), Fairfield 873m (2,864ft), Hart Crag 822m (2,697ft), Dove Crag 792m (2,598ft), Little Hart Crag 637m (2,090ft)
Distance:	14km (9 miles) via Hartsop above How, 16km (10 miles) via High Hartsop Dodd
Navigation:	Moderate
Terrain:	Easy
Winter:	Difficult
Map:	Harveys 1:25,000 Superwalker: Eastern Lakeland. OS 1:25,000 Outdoor Leisure 5 and 7: The English Lakes – North-Eastern area and South-Eastern area

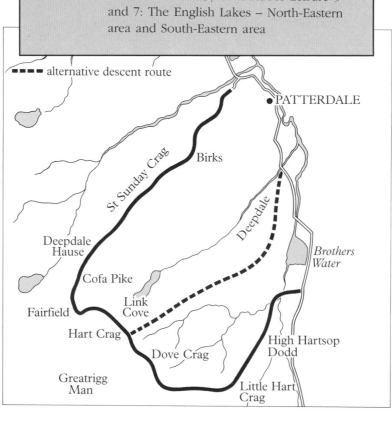

Fairfield is a great hulk of a mountain sitting at the centre of a number of fine ridges. The well-known Fairfield Horseshoe starts to the south and takes in the ridges either side of Rydal Beck. It is an excellent walk but it does not reveal the finest aspects of Fairfield. The southern and western slopes are steep but mostly grassy and regular, with only a few small crags. The east side is completely different. At the head of Deepdale and Dovedale lie great cliffs, rough screes and a tangle of complex, rugged terrain. From the west Fairfield is a big hill, from the east it is a mountain.

On the east side there are two other horseshoe routes. The shorter one is the circuit of Deepdale from St Sunday Crag to Hartsop above How. The greater horseshoe takes in Dovedale as well and finishes on High Hartsop Dodd. Both, to my mind, are superior to the better-known horseshoe to the west.

Personal experiences colour any view on the hills, so perhaps I should admit to two very different ones that may have affected my opinion of the western side of Fairfield. On the first occasion I set off with a friend from Grasmere to do the western half of the horseshoe and then descend via Grisedale Hause. To reach the ridge we slogged straight up the steep slopes of Greatrigg Man. It was the middle of a heatwave and the sun was hammering down, and when we finally reached the summit we were sweat-sodden, exhausted and desperately thirsty. This was in my early hillwalking days and for some reason I can no longer remember (forgetfulness, laziness, ignorance, stupidity?) we were not carrying water bottles, although we did have an orange each. I watched my companion eat his and then began to peel mine, only to see black putrid liquid oozing out. The whole orange was rotten. At the time I believed those who said it was dangerous to drink from streams on the fells, so I ignored the waters of Tongue Gill on the descent. My mouth felt disgusting and I was swaying with dehydration when we reached Grasmere. Dashing into the first pub we came to, I immediately downed two pints of chilled shandy. Freezing

Sunset over the Fairfield Fells from Hartsop above How.

Ullswater in summer.

liquid, over-heated body – the results were predictable. It all came back up again within seconds.

The other experience relates to too much water rather than too little. Four of us had set off, intent on walking the whole length of the Helvellyn and Fairfield ranges. It was fine to Grisedale Tarn, but there dark clouds and the first spots of rain suggested a change in the weather. Two of the party, sensibly, descended to Grasmere. Two of us went on. By the time we were on the summit of Fairfield the rain was lashing down and we could see nothing. The rain continued all the way down the Dove Crag ridge and we were in thick cloud the whole way, only emerging from it a short way above Ambleside.

The dramatic landscape is the real reason for preferring the eastern side of these hills, of course. It is not noticeably drier! Which is the best way to do the alternative horseshoe depends on whether you prefer to have a long walk-in or a long walk-out. I generally prefer the latter and it does have the advantage here that a decision as to which version of the horseshoe to do does not have to be made until late in the day, when you can see what the weather is like and how tired you feel.

The path to St Sunday Crag starts from the minor road that runs up the south side of lower Grisedale and climbs steadily to Birks, the top at the east end of the fell. The ridge then undulates west for a kilometre before the final steeper ascent to the summit.

As well as being an impressive hill in its own right, St Sunday Crag is a superb viewpoint for the Helvellyn range. Straight across Grisedale is Striding Edge, usually with a long line of tiny silhouetted figures dancing along the crest. Several times I have shared St Sunday Crag with just a few others, while crowds can be seen on Helvellyn.

There is a good view down Ullswater too, perhaps the best reason for doing the horseshoe the other way round. The view ahead is also impressive, with the dark crags of Fairfield's north-east face rising from aptly named Deepdale. These stretch for about 2km (1¼ miles) east of the summit, with the huge buttress of Greenhow End dominant.

From St Sunday Crag the path drops down to Deepdale Hause, beyond which is the steep, stony ridge of Cofa Pike. The ascent of this is easy, although I always feel nervous here when I look down the drops to either side, remembering an occasion when I descended the ridge at speed on my backside. This took place on one of my first-ever fell walks, a school outing from Grasmere to Patterdale. Snow lay on the ground and Deepdale Hause was hidden by thick mist, as were the steep drops all around. The teacher in charge peered down into the mirk and then turned to me. 'Townsend', he commanded, 'slide down there and see if it's safe.' I was too young, too ignorant and not yet rebellious enough to disobey. I also assumed it must be safe, so down I slid. Once I had survived, the rest of the party, some 20 strong, sat down and slid after me. I shudder to think of the results if the teacher's navigation had not been accurate or if the snow had been harder and icier and I had shot over the edge. I cannot remember how I felt at the time, but the memory is frightening.

Fairfield is only a short though rough and stony walk from Cofa Pike. When you reach the summit good navigation is needed, as it is flat and featureless and there are so many cairns that they hinder rather than help with finding the way off. In clear weather the edge of the cliffs can be followed round to Hart Crag, with dramatic views into Deepdale in places. There is a path some way back from the edge that is safer and easier in mist. The shorter horseshoe heads north-east from Hart Crag along the ridge to Hartsop above How and then down to the road a couple of kilometres south of Patterdale. There are excellent views of the crags rimming Link Cove to the north-east of Hart Crag on this descent.

The greater horseshoe continues south to Dove Crag. At the col before the summit there is a way to the east that drops down past the massive overhanging cliff, one of the most impressive pieces of rock in the Lake District, that gives the fell its name. A diversion here is well worthwhile. If you do not want to climb back up you can continue on down Dovedale.

Near the top of the crag there is a roomy cave that can be reached by an easy traverse across rough slopes. Two of us stayed in the cave one rainy night and found it quite comfortable. Until, that is, an organized party of about a dozen teenagers moved in with us. Their instructor set up a bivi tent right on the edge of the cave and hid himself in it. It quickly became clear that they did not know how their stoves worked or how best to sort out their gear for the night. As their instructor was clearly not going to re-emerge, we took on his role for the evening. The cave is an impressive place to spend the night, with a view out into space to the east. I imagine sunrise from here must be spectacular. All we saw at dawn was heavy rain.

Dove Crag is where the south arm of the greater horseshoe heads east over the summit of Little Hart Crag and then down a narrow ridge to High Hartsop Dodd. The views of Dove Crag, Hoggett Gill and Dovedale from this ridge are superb. A final steep descent leads to the foot of Dovedale just south of Brothers Water.

ALONG THE HELVELLYN RIDGE

Helvellyn is a two-faced hill, a sort of Jekyll and Hyde
piece of geography: all green and verdurous to forest-
choked Thirlmere on the west and cove-bitten on the east.

Hamish Brown, *Hamish's Groats End Walk*

Start/finish:	Patterdale/Glenridding
Summits:	Raise 883m (2,897ft), White Side 863m (2,831ft), Helvellyn 950m (3,117ft), Nethermost Pike 891m (2,923ft), Dollywagon Pike 858m (2,815ft)
Distance:	18km (11 miles)
Navigation:	Easy
Terrain:	Moderate
Winter:	Difficult
Maps:	Harveys 1:25,000 Superwalker: Eastern Lakeland. OS 1:25,000 Outdoor Leisure 5: The English Lakes – North-Eastern area

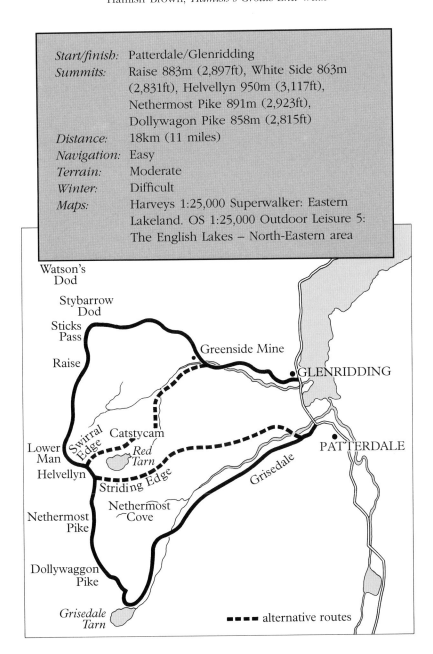

Watson's Dod
Stybarrow Dod
Sticks Pass
Raise
Greenside Mine
GLENRIDDING
Swirral Edge
Catstycam
Red Tarn
Lower Man
PATTERDALE
Helvellyn
Striding Edge
Grisedale
Nethermost Cove
Nethermost Pike
Dollywaggon Pike
Grisedale Tarn

▬ ▬ ▬ ▬ alternative routes

Helvellyn is probably the most climbed fell in the Lake District, and Striding Edge is certainly the most popular route to its top. The traverse of this narrow arete is exciting, but it is usually so crowded that the feelings engendered by the hills – awe, joy, calm, solitude, loss of self into nature – are lost and the point of being there is gone. The last time I was on Striding Edge, on a cold winter's day, a continuous line of walkers spread along its length and we had to queue several times. I vowed then never to go this way again unless at midnight on a weekday in November. It is no longer a classic walk because of the numbers who go there and I am afraid I cannot recommend it.

Most of those who go up Striding Edge go down Swirral Edge across the Red Tarn basin to the north. Few, however, continue on to Catstycam at the eastern end of the spur down which Swirral Edge runs, yet this steep-sided tiny summit is one of the best viewpoints for Striding Edge, Red Tarn and the east face of Helvellyn.

Another concern I have about Striding and Swirral Edges is to do with safety. Both are rough walks with big drops on either side, rather than scrambles. In summer they are reasonably safe. This, combined with dramatic situations and a feeling of seriousness, attracts many people with little experience of rocky terrain. Even in summer, unsure and unhappy walkers can be found clinging to rocks along both edges. In winter, however, snow and ice can turn the round of the edges from a fell walk to a mountaineering expedition, a very easy one admittedly but still requiring skill with ice axe and crampons. People who find the edges hard to cope with in summer will find them far more so and far more dangerous in winter, but they still come. On my last visit I was horrified at how many people were not carrying ice axe or crampons. I was also shocked on the initial steep descent of Swirral Edge to see people sliding down a slope of hard, icy snow on their backsides, despite the steep drops to either side. This is not paranoia on my part. Unsurprisingly, winter accidents are not uncommon here, and at times the national park have resorted to putting a ranger at the start of the Striding Edge path to warn people of the conditions above.

One of the best-known winter accidents occurred long ago in 1805, when a man named Charles Gough fell some 180m (600ft) from Striding Edge towards Red Tarn. His body was not discovered until three months later, his dog still sitting beside the remains. This was viewed as an amazing act of loyalty at the time. A consideration as to how the dog survived so long results in a different explanation, however. Sir Walter Scott and William Wordsworth, who climbed Helvellyn together in 1805, both wrote poems on the accident. The main reason it is still remembered though is the presence of the Gough Memorial Stone, erected in 1890, near the top of Striding Edge.

Fortunately, there are other excellent walks on Helvellyn. The main south–north running ridge is the largest area of high land in England. For over 8km (5 miles) this broad, massive ridge does not drop below 750m (2,400ft). To the west the sides fall away in even slopes of grass and scree to Thirlmere. Ascents from here are steep and, except for a few gill scrambles, not particularly interesting. On the west, though, a series of cliff-rimmed coves takes great chunks out of the ridge and the scene is wild and mountainous. The best ascents, then, are from this side and the best walking on the ridge is along the eastern rim.

There are many ways on to the ridge from the east, but one of the best rounds is from Grisedale to Sticks Gill. The walk up Grisedale from the road just south of Ullswater is easy and scenic, with the steep slopes of St Sunday Crag to the south and the rugged heads of Nethermost and Ruthwaite Coves to the north-west. Grisedale Tarn lies at the head of the valley, just below Grisedale Hause. This was once a pack-horse route between Patterdale and Grasmere.

There are good campsites around Grisedale Tarn, but I would avoid them in stormy weather as they are very exposed. I had one of my worst nights on a mountain here, when unexpected high winds and lashing rain rushed in from the west after dark. My lightweight backpacking tent shook so violently with each gust that I got dressed, packed up all my gear and held on to the poles. The blasts got stronger and

stronger until a pole snapped with a loud crack. Bundling the tent into the pack, I set off for Grisedale Hause and Grasmere, only to find that walking into the wind was almost impossible. Realizing I was exhausting myself without making any progress, I turned and let the wind blow me down Grisedale. There was no shelter anywhere and I arrived in Patterdale at about 4am very tired and very wet. The wind was still blowing hard down there, so there was no point in trying to erect a damaged tent. I ended up curled up for the last few hours of the night on the floor of a cubicle in a public convenience. It was an exceptional storm though – the same one, as I later learnt, that caused havoc out in the Atlantic to the Fastnet Yacht Race.

From the tarn, a wide path leads north up to Dollywagon Pike and on over Nethermost Pike to Helvellyn. This is a good route in mist but in clear

Striding Edge and Red Tarn from Catstycam.

weather sticking to the edge of the crags to the east is far superior, as it gives tremendous views down to Ruthwaite and Nethermost Coves and across to Striding Edge. It is also surprisingly unpopular: most walkers seem very reluctant to leave cairned paths. I walked this edge one August bank holiday and met hardly anyone, although I could hear voices on the path most of the time and the summit of Helvellyn was almost buried in bodies.

The bare, stony top of Helvellyn gives comprehensive views of the Lakeland fells but, as so often, the best ones are close by, namely the view to

the east of Swirral and Striding Edges curving round above the dark waters of Red Tarn. The summit can be a windy place. I lost my balaclava here one cold November day when a gust of wind sent it whirling high into space over Red Tarn. Even with my hood up, my ears burned with cold and my head ached, forcing me to abandon my high-level walk and descend quickly. Ever since, I have carried two hats in winter. On another occasion the wind was so strong that reaching the summit cairn, which perches on the edge of the drop to the east, was quite difficult. Once there, we felt in great danger of being blown down to Red Tarn and we

Glenridding in autumn.

quickly moved away from the edge, having to lean into the wind to make any progress.

We discovered the disorientating effects that wind and mist can have a short while later as we descended to the south. A group of people were huddled on the col with Nethermost Pike. They greeted us with a startling question: 'This is the top, isn't it?' 'Well, um, no,' we replied, awkwardly – for it seemed apparent to us that they were in a dip and we weren't quite sure how to respond to such a seemingly bizarre query – 'it's up there.' We indicated the slopes we had just descended and hurried on. Mist can affect people's perception of slope angles and the size of objects, while strong winds can make thinking clearly difficult. The combination of snow and mist is even worse, and I have been reduced to throwing snowballs ahead of me at times. If the snowball appears to stop in mid-air there is a slope ahead; if it lands below you there is a descent; if it disappears, back away quickly – you could be on the edge of a cliff or out on a cornice.

Watching the sunrise from a mountaintop is always a magical experience. Helvellyn is one of the best summits for this, as the view east is unimpeded by any higher hills and the glow of the still-hidden sun fills the whole sky from north to south, before the first red edge appears in the far distance and light floods in on you.

Midsummer's night is a favourite one to spend out on Helvellyn. You will not be alone, but the dawn can still be wonderful – if the sky is clear, of course. Many years ago I spent the night on the summit with a friend after an ascent via Catstycam and Swirral Edge. The few hours of darkness were spent bivouacking in the summit shelter. At first we were alone, but as the first

faint strip of light began to appear in the east voices could be heard approaching.

By the time the sunrise really began a dozen or so people were pacing up and down the summit, trying to keep warm in the surprisingly cold air. Then the horizon turned orange and red and rays of light began to pick out the details of the hitherto black mass of land below us. Bathed in a golden glow that gradually faded as the sun appeared and strengthened, the fells were sharp and distinct, far more real than they would appear in the hot haze of midday. It was a glorious dawn. Even the lone but loud voice of an American woman telling everyone to 'look at that' could not spoil it.

From Helvellyn the ridge path continues over White Side and Raise to Sticks Pass, at 750m (2,450ft) the lowest point between Grisedale Tarn and the northern end of the ridge. Beyond Sticks Pass are the Dodds, pleasant rounded grassy hills but without the mountainous features found to the south. The walking on them is unexciting, but they are ideal for cross-country skiing.

From Sticks Pass a good path descends Sticks Gill East into the Greenside lead-mining area. On the right can be seen the ski hut and ski tow belonging to the Lake District Ski Club, placed here because this shallow bowl on the north-east slopes of Raise holds the snow well. Thank goodness the winters here are not snowy enough for further encroachments of this pernicious mountain-destroying, industrial mass pursuit into the fells.

On the descent there are signs of mining everywhere and the main mine, in use until 1959, is reached at the head of Glenridding Beck. One of the old buildings is now a youth hostel. The road from the hostel leads down to Glenridding.

HIGH STREET AND THE KENTMERE HORSESHOE

*Ill Bell, Rainsborrow Crag, High Street and opposite High
Street Harter Fell, with the Nan Bield Pass between the
two, . . . are quite able to supply a respectable
programme of fell walking.*

John B. Barber & George Atkinson, *Lakeland Passes*

Start/finish:	Kentmere
Summits:	Yoke 706m (2,316ft), Ill Bell 757m (2,483ft), Froswick 720m (2,362ft), Thornthwaite Crag 784m (2,572ft), High Street 828m (2,717ft), Mardale Ill Bell 761m (2,496ft), Harter Fell 778m (2,552ft), Kentmere Pike 730m (2,395ft)
Distance:	16km (10 miles)
Navigation:	Moderate
Terrain:	Easy
Winter:	Difficult
Map:	Harveys 1:25,000 Superwalker: Eastern Lakeland. OS 1:25,000 Outdoor Leisure 5 and 7: The English Lakes – North-Eastern area and South-Eastern area

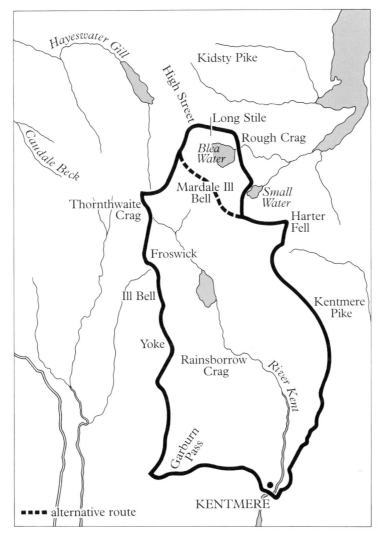

Left: *The High
Street ridge from
Riggindale.*

The High Street ridge follows the same
pattern, on a slightly smaller scale, as
the Helvellyn–Fairfield ridge just to the
west. The western slopes are again
generally smooth and crag free, while
the eastern side is rugged and rough
with narrow spurs, deep coves and
dramatic crags. The area has a character
of its own of course, and there are
many fine walks here. Also, while
nowhere in the Lake District can be
said to be little frequented except
perhaps the hills north of Skiddaw
and Blencathra, High Street and its
neighbouring hills are less visited than
those to the west.

Although the summits are not quite
as high as those to the west, the High
Street ridge is the longest high ridge in
the Lakes. For 13km (8 miles), from
Yoke in the south to Loadpot Hill in the
north, the ridge stays above 610m
(2,000ft). Walking the whole length of
the ridge is challenging and enjoyable.
It misses some of the finest scenery in
the area though, and the northern end
is not that interesting as it mainly
consists of rolling moorland.

There are a number of horseshoe
walks in the area, of which the best is
undoubtedly the Kentmere Horseshoe.
This can easily be extended to include

High Street. The walk begins in Kentmere and initially heads west to Garburn Pass on an old track that links Kentmere with Troutbeck.

Garburn Pass is where I first learnt that people from far away (and that can mean southern England as well as abroad) may have startling misconceptions about the Lakeland hills, misconceptions that could lead them into danger. Late on an autumn afternoon as I descended from a day on High Street, I met two women with large rucksacks at the pass heading up. I wondered where they were going with only an hour or so of daylight left. 'Oh, we're going to camp at Thornthwaite Crag,' they replied in accents that suggested they were American. 'Not easy to pitch a tent up there,' I said, thinking of the small stony summit. 'Oh, we haven't got a tent.' A stove and water? No again. We'll light a fire, they said. I began to realize that perhaps they weren't familiar with the Lake District. I failed, however, to convince them that there wouldn't be trees at

'only 2,570 feet', nor that it would be cold and might be wet. Their map was a half-inch to the mile one unsuitable for hill use, and they were intending to go on to Patterdale. As they strode off up the path I continued down, hoping that the weather would stay clear and dry.

Yoke, the first peak on the walk, lies directly north of the pass on the good path that runs the length of the ridge. The top is grassy and rounded, giving no hint of the tremendous 915m (3,000ft) cliff of Rainsborrow Crag to the east.

The next peak, Ill Bell, is easily identifiable from afar due to its distinctive pyramidal shape. The summit is small and rocky with a collection of tall cairns, and the view of Windermere stretching away towards Morecambe Bay is excellent. The rise and fall of the ridge continues to Froswick, another cone-shaped fell, then on to Thornthwaite Crag, which has an impressive 4m (14ft) slender cairn on the top visible from afar. This peak stands in a complex area of fells and

High Street from the start of the ascent via Long Stile.

there are views down two north-running valleys – Threshthwaite Glen and Hayeswater Gill – and two south-running ones – Kentmere and Trout Beck.

Leaving Kentmere behind, it is now an easy stroll north-west to High Street. The summit is featureless and empty apart from a wall running across it, but it has more of a history than almost any other in Lakeland. It is most famous for the Roman road that ran along the summit linking the forts at Ambleside (Galava) and Brougham (Brocavum), a total distance of 40km (25 miles). This was built in the first century AD, but there may have been a road here already. Much more recently, local shepherds used to meet annually on High Street to exchange sheep that had strayed. This became something of a social occasion, and wrestling matches and horse races were held (hence the alternative name of Racecourse Hill). These meets ceased in 1835.

While one can imagine the Roman legions tramping by and the thunder of horses' hooves and the cheering of the shepherds, there isn't actually much to see. Just to the east, though, lie steep, craggy slopes and below them the deepest tarn in the Lake District, Blea Tarn, into which the slopes continue down for some 60m (200ft). This impressive scene can be viewed from the Long Stile–Rough Crag ridge, which starts north-east of the summit and is well worth the diversion. Long Stile itself is a narrow, rocky arete leading down to a gap in the ridge known as Caspel Gate. To the north is equally wild and rugged Riggindale, with the sharp peak of Kidsty Pike rising on the far side. The ridge descends to the despoiled valley of Mardale with its ugly reservoir, once the lake of Haweswater. In dry summers the walls and buildings of Mardale re-emerge from the water.

Perhaps one day the dam will be torn down and the valley restored. Until then this is a valley I prefer not to visit.

If you do drop down Long Stile rather than climb back up, you can descend to Blea Tarn and then work a way round to dramatically situated Small Water and Nan Bield Pass. I once took this route inadvertently when I stopped for a rest near Caspel Gate. Looking for something in my rucksack, I unpacked some of my gear, including the stove. This was a Trangia, a model that combines the burner with a pan set and is shaped like a thick disc or wheel. Somehow I knocked it on to its side and it began to roll down the hillside. I watched as it picked up speed and bounced into the air off several boulders before vanishing from view. Although convinced I would never find it, and if I did it would be smashed to bits, I set off down to look for it. Almost down at the tarn I finally located it, wedged between two rocks. Apart from a few dents it was unharmed.

The Long Stile–Blea Tarn–Nan Bield Pass route passes through superb scenery but bypasses the peak of Mardale Ill Bell. If you want to climb this peak – really just a minor top of High Street and omitted as a separate summit from the Nuttall's Mountains of England because it rises only 10m (35ft) from the col with High Street (their criterion is a rise of 15m/50ft) – it lies about ½km (¼ mile) and 140m (450ft) to the north-west. Nan Bield is a narrow, rocky notch of a pass, from which you can descend to Kentmere if time or energy is running out.

Otherwise, the eastern arm of the Kentmere Horseshoe still remains. Two summits are involved, Harter Fell and Kentmere Pike, linked by first a fence and then a wall, before a path angles down to Kentmere.

BLENCATHRA AND SKIDDAW

*The many buttresses and gullies present probably the
greatest variety of routes to the summit of any fell.*

John & Anne Nuttall, *The Mountains of England & Wales*

Start/finish:	Threlkeld/Scales to Keswick
Summits:	Blencathra 868m (2,848ft), Skiddaw 931m (3,054ft)
Distance:	16km (10 miles)
Navigation:	Moderate
Terrain:	Difficult
Winter:	Very difficult
Map:	Harveys 1:25,000 Superwalker: Northern Lakeland

Blencathra and Skiddaw dominate the landscape to the north of Keswick and the A66, and are well seen on approaches from Penrith to the east and from the south. Attitudes to the two mountains differ greatly, however. Skiddaw is often regarded as a mere lump, a mound of a hill that just happens to be over 915m (3,000ft) high, while Blencathra is highly praised. While I agree Blencathra is a fine mountain, I like Skiddaw too. Both are worth climbing and it is not difficult to combine the ascents. Blencathra presents its finest face to the south and has two superb ways to the summit, while the rather dull standard way up Skiddaw from Keswick is partly the reason many people have such a poor opinion of it. A round of the two is best started, then, with Blencathra.

The south face of Blencathra consists of three ridges, each one finishing in a steep buttress, with deep ravines between them and two large buttresses at either end. All are called fells, the ridges being Gategill Fell, Hall's Fell and Doddick Fell, and the enclosing buttresses Blease Fell and Scales Fell. Appropriately, the summit lies right at the top of the central ridge, Hall's Fell, and used to be known as Hallsfell Top. These ridges make up the classic view of Blencathra when seen from the east, and under snow give the mountain an alpine appearance that belies its height. All can be used for ascent, as can the gullies, but the finest way up by far is Hall's Fell. So good is this that Wainwright describes it as '*positively* the finest way to any mountaintop in the district'.

However, hidden from view round to the east, though visible on approaches from Penrith, is the rocky crest known as Sharp Edge. This is the narrowest, most dramatic such arete in the Lakes, far surpassing Striding Edge on Helvellyn. It too is a superb route to Blencathra and is often combined with Hall's Fell as an excellent if short round.

Whichever ascent route is chosen, it

should be noted that both are steep and have exposed sections and can be tricky in winter conditions. Indeed, both are graded winter climbs, Hall's Fell being a Grade 1 and Sharp Edge a 1/2. Ice axe and crampons are essential and a rope may well be welcome on Sharp Edge. I certainly found one so on one winter ascent.

The hamlet of Threlkeld is the starting point for Hall's Fell. The initial path goes past Gategill, where there is an old lead mine, Blencathra once being heavily mined. From here Hall's Fell soars above, rising 700m (2,300ft) in less than 2km (1¼ miles). To begin with the route climbs the steep heather-clad slopes of the lower buttress, but this

soon tapers to the upper ridge, which is rocky and excitingly narrow. A path avoids most of the difficulties, but the best route stays right on the crest where the scrambling is not hard but the situation is sensational. Far below on either side are Gate Gill and Doddick Gill. Hall's Fell ends perfectly right on the summit of Blencathra.

Sharp Edge, the other best route to the top (and I am not going to choose between them), is reached from Scales by the path up Mousthwaite Comb, then beside the River Glenderamackin and Scales Beck to the dark, shaded waters of Scales Tarn. From here the serrated crest of Sharp Edge, ending in the steep cliff of Foule Crag, looks very

Skiddaw from the Newlands valley.

spectacular. It is not that long or difficult, but it is very exposed and not a place to be in a strong wind. There is a narrow path just below the crest. Harder than the actual edge, in my view, is the final very steep scramble up the overlapping slates of Foule Crag. Once up, a short walk leads south to the summit.

To the south the whole of Lakeland can be seen, while to the east Cross Fell and the Northern Pennines are in view, but if the weather is cold or windy you will not want to linger long as there is no shelter of any sort, the summit cairn being no more than a small pile of slate. A curiosity is a white quartzite cross laid out on the turf near the top

of Foule Crag. This was originally built in the 1940s as a memorial to a man who died on the fells, but was enlarged extensively in following years by a Threlkeld man called Harold Robinson.

The bulk of Skiddaw can be seen clearly to the west. To reach it, head north then east across the flat, boggy expanse of Mungrisdale Common towards the remote youth hostel of Skiddaw House. To the north the rolling, Pennine-like hills known as the Back O'Skiddaw fade into the horizon. From Skiddaw House a direct ascent of Skiddaw can be made. The hillside is rough, but there are no crags and it is only steep near the top.

Skiddaw's stony summit is about 1km (⅔ mile) long. There are several tops, the one with the trig point near the northern end being the highest. Because it is an easy top to reach, a friend of mine left Skiddaw to last when he was climbing all the Lakeland 610m (2,000ft) tops. He also chose to climb it on New Year's Day. The summit was in mist with a cool wind blowing as we gathered round drinking wine out of real wine glasses and eating cake to celebrate. Other walkers loomed out of the mist and passed by looking somewhat startled. I half expected them to return to check that they really had seen what they thought they had seen.

In clear weather there is an extensive view of the Lakeland fells to the south, while to the north can be seen the Solway Firth and the Southern Uplands of Scotland. The best view though is, as always, much nearer and that is the one down to Keswick and along Derwent Water.

The wide tourist path, in use since the last century, leads easily down the broad south-east slopes of Skiddaw to Keswick.

FIVE

THE SCOTTISH HIGHLANDS

THE wide-open spaces of the Cairngorms; the deep, narrow glens of Knoydart; the great cliffs of Glen Coe and Ben Nevis; the rock ridges of the Cuillin; the surreal peaks of the far north-west; the sinuous sea lochs of the western seaboard; the scattered remnants of ancient pine forest; the bogs of Rannoch Moor; the tallest peaks, the deepest lakes, the highest waterfalls, the wildest country – the Highlands have it all.

The scale of the land is much greater than anywhere to the south. The glens are longer, the hills higher, the whole landscape vaster. This can lead to confusion for first-time walkers and it can take time to get used to the distances involved. The size makes walking here more serious too: it can be a long way to anywhere. Winters are snowier and colder than to the south. This is the nearest to real wilderness we have in Britain and as such it is the finest walking country by far.

Selecting ten walks out of the many hundreds of fine ones is an impossible task. There are many essential ones I have had to omit. An Teallach, Beinn Eighe, Aonach Eagach, Bla Bheinn, Ladhar Bheinn, Quinag, Ben Alder, Ben Lui, Buchaille Etive Mor . . . the list goes on. Here I have just tried to give a taste of the variety of hill walks available in the Highlands.

BIDEAN NAM BIAN

The head of the valley was dominated by an unclimbed buttress of the summit ridge, two thousand feet above. All along the western wall icy turrets and battlements caught the sun, gleamed and shone.

W.H. Murray, *Mountaineering in Scotland*

Start/finish:	Glen Coe – Achnambeithach to Allt-na-reigh
Summits:	Bidean nam Bian 1,150m (3,766ft), Stob Coire nam Beith 1,107m (3,621ft), Stob Coire nan Lochan 1,115m (3,657ft), Stob Coire Sgreamhach 1,072m (3,497ft)
Distance:	14.5km (9 miles)
Navigation:	Difficult
Terrain:	Difficult
Winter:	Difficult
Map:	Harveys 1:25,000 Superwalker: Glen Coe

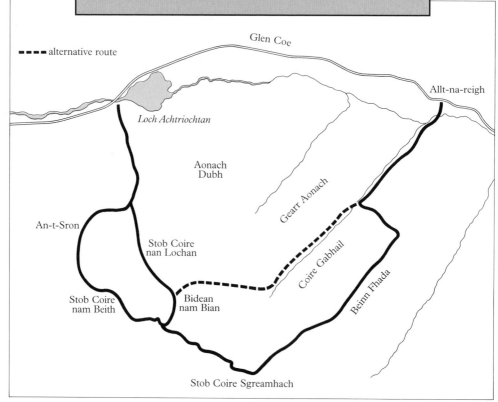

This is a magnificent mountain, one of the finest in Britain. With subsidiary peaks that would be mountains in their own right elsewhere, high corries, hidden valleys, massive cliffs, superb ridges and several streams, it is virtually a whole range in itself. This is summed up in the name, which translates as 'the peak or the chief of the mountains' (Bian being a corruption of Beann).

For such a big, high hill the summit of Bidean nam Bian is surprisingly hard to see from below. On the Glen Coe side it is shielded from view by the massive crag-fringed buttresses of the Three Sisters, truncated spurs that run north from the main ridge. From the upper end of Glen Coe the famous view of these three ridges – Beinn Fhada, Gearr Aonach and Aonach Dubh – makes them look like separate summits. To appreciate Bidean in full you have to see it from on high, from the Mamores, say, or the Aonach Eagach, or, ideally, by walking its length and its ridges.

Bidean is a Glen Coe peak and all the best ascents are from that side. Over the years Glen Coe has had the image of being a gloomy place full of foreboding, as though the famous massacre that happened here has cast a pall over the glen. If everywhere horrific acts have happened in the past carried the burden of them through the centuries there would be few cheerful places in Britain! No, Glen Coe can be grim and cheerless in lashing rain and low cloud, but then so can anywhere. In sunshine it is a glorious glen, full of light and colour, a place that lifts the spirits rather than depresses them, and in snow it has an awe-inspiring, big-mountain feel.

What has damaged Glen Coe, though not destroyed it, is, ironically, the National Trust for Scotland, who own the land on both sides of the glen. It was bequeathed to them by Percy

Unna, a pioneer of wild land conservation, in the 1930s. Unna laid down a set of guidelines for the management of mountain areas, now known as Unna's Rules, which say that while there should be unrestricted access to the hills they should not be made easier to climb and no signposts, cairns or other waymarks should be erected or new paths constructed. In Glen Coe, though, bridges and signposts have been put up by the Trust and a visitor centre built. There are

Previous pages:
Cornices curling
over the edge of
Braeriach.

On the ascent of
Bidean nam Bian
with the Aonach
Eagach on the
skyline.

signs that the Trust are becoming aware of the effects of their developments and it looks as though the visitor centre will be relocated in Glencoe village, where it should have been sited in the first place.

Unna set down his rules long before hillwalking and climbing became mass pursuits. Today their application is even more necessary if the 'primitive state' of the hills, as Unna put it, is to be maintained. In the USA and Canada, where I have done thousands of kilometres of mountain walking, such guidelines are standard in designated wilderness areas. The same should apply throughout the British hills, especially the Highlands, whoever owns the land and whether or not it is included in any present or future national parks or other conservation areas. As it is, only the John Muir Trust, named for another wilderness pioneer little known in his homeland, is committed to managing wild areas without promotion or development.

To return to Bidean nam Bian. The western end of the mountain is dominated by the fine pointed peaks of Stob Coire nam Beith and Stob Coire nan Lochan. These can be reached from the southern end of Loch Achtriochtan in lower Glen Coe by the path beside the Allt Coire nam Beithach, which tumbles down a ravine between Aonach Dubh and An t-Sron. Once into the spectacular upper corrie there are two choices. You can go right and climb steep scree to the ridge between An t-Sron and Stob Coire nam Beith, and then go up the last and on to Bidean itself. While this is a fine route, the one to the left is even better. This climbs up steep slopes through stupendous rock scenery to the col between Stob Coire nan Lochan and

Bidean. Both peaks can be reached easily from the col. The two huge cliffs below the summit of Bidean seen on the way up are the famous (among climbers) Diamond and Church Door Buttresses.

The summit of Bidean is small and neat, perched at the junction of three narrow ridges. The views are impressive, especially that to the north over the Aonach Eagach to Ben Nevis. The summit ridge runs south-east to the head of Coire Gabhail and then up to Stob Coire Sgreamhach. From here you can scramble out along the Beinn Fhada spur, with the great flat-bottomed defile of Coire Gabhail on your left. The spur ends in cliffs, however, so at some point a way needs to be picked carefully down the steep slopes into Coire Gabhail.

The corrie is a magnificent place. Hidden from the road by a narrow boulder-choked ravine, this huge hanging valley is popularly known as the Lost Valley, although this is hardly accurate any more as there is a clear path from the road across the bridge which the NTS have sadly built across the River Coe. In *Mountaineering in Scotland*, Murray writes of the river that the 'fifteen-mile length bars access to the mountain and helps to preserve the Lost Valley's sanctity' and that it is 'sullied by no bridge hereabouts'. It is now.

Once through the ravine, Coire Gabhail widens out into a long, grassy meadow walled by crags and high peaks. It is a dramatic and inspirational place. The name means Corrie of Booty, referring to the hiding here of stolen cattle. The easiest way to Bidean, although still steep and stony, is by climbing to the col between the summit and Stob Coire nan Lochan.

THE MAMORES

One of the great hill days in Scotland.
Roger Smith, *Classic Walks in Scotland*

Start/finish:	Glen Nevis
Summits:	Binnein Beag 940m (3,083ft), Sgurr Eilde Mor 1,000m (3,279ft), Binnein Mor 1,128m (3,700ft), Na Gruagaichean 1,050m (3,442ft), An Gearanach 985m (3,230ft), Stob Coire a'Chairn 983m (3,219ft), Am Bodach 1,032m (3,382ft), Sgor an Iubhair 1,001m (3,284ft), Sgurr a'Mhaim 1,099m (3,601ft), Stob Ban 999m (3,274ft), Mullach nan Coirean 939m (3,077ft)
Distance:	35km (22 miles)
Navigation:	Difficult
Terrain:	Moderate
Winter:	Difficult
Map:	Harveys 1:25,000 Superwalker: Ben Nevis

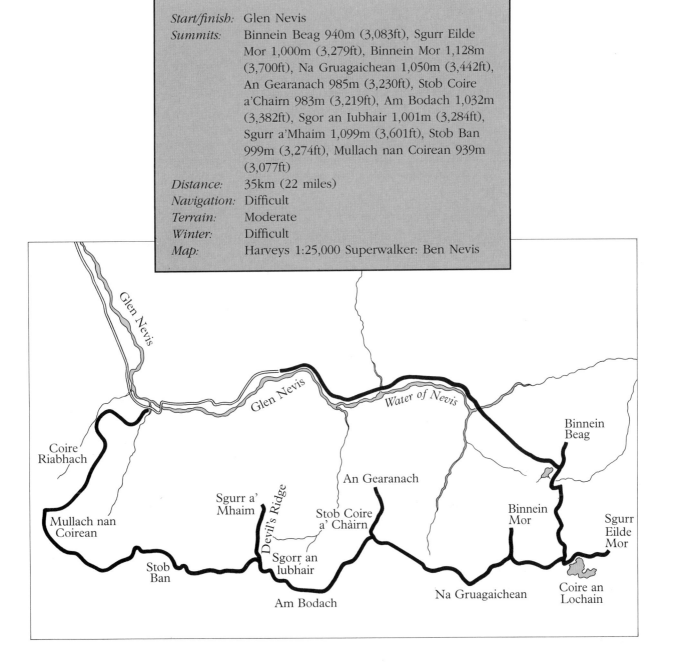

On the journey down Glen Nevis a splendid view opens up of big, pale, conical hills rising above the rich woodlands. These are the central peaks on the ridge known as the Mamores, that separates Glen Nevis from Loch Leven to the south. One of the longest and most impressive high-level ridges in Britain, the Mamores crest is 11km (7 miles) long and never drops below 740m (2,425ft). Eight Munros lie on the main ridge, while two more are to be found on northern projecting spurs and a final one out on its own to the east. While all of these can be climbed individually or in groups on circular walks from the north or south, the best way to do them by far is in one long traverse, a traverse that is probably the best ridge walk in Britain.

The Mamores are steep, sharp-topped hills linked by narrow ridges and cut into by wild, lonely corries, especially to the north. The walking is generally on grass or flat stones, and although often steep there are only a couple of short sections of easy scrambling. In winter, however, cornices and avalanche-prone slopes can make the hills dangerous.

The traverse of the whole ridge is lengthy and involves around 3,000m (10,000ft) of ascent – 12 hours is a good time for a strong walker. This, however, is only the first half of a walk first done in June 1964 by Philip Tranter and hence known as Tranter's Walk. After the Mamores he returned to Glen Nevis youth hostel via the Grey Corries, the Aonachs and Ben Nevis, to give a total of 18 Munros, 56km (35 miles) and 6,000m (20,000ft) of ascent – and all within 24 hours. The record for this round is held by Mark McDermott, who ran it in an astonishing 12 hours 50 minutes in 1990. As if Tranter's Walk wasn't long enough, in 1978 Charlie Ramsey created Ramsey's Round by

Binnein Mor from Binnein Beag.

*On the Mamores
ridge between Stob
Coire a'Chairn
and Am Bodach.*

going on to add the five Munros around Loch Treig, along with another 32km (20 miles) and 2,400m (8,000ft) of ascent. It took him just two minutes under 24 hours. Most hillgoers will be happy enough with just the Mamores.

My first attempt to walk the Mamores in one day was on a Great Outdoors Challenge crossing of Scotland. This meant I was going from west to east, the hardest way, and had a heavy pack loaded with enough food to see me to Dalwhinnie, six days away. It didn't help that I had walked 38.5km (24 miles) the previous day, either. All this is by way of excusing my failure to complete the ridge. I made it as far as An Gearanach before descending to Glen Nevis. According to my journal, *en route* I admired the 'grand ridge to Stob Ban' and the impressive east face of the same peak, had good views of Bidean nam Bian, Ben Nevis and the Grey Corries, stocked up on water at Lochan Coire nam Miseach, found the Devil's Ridge out to Sgurr a'Mhaim exciting and

airy 'with a couple of awkward moves', but the descent from Am Bodach 'nasty' due to the steepness and loose scree (I guess I was tiring by then) and the ridge out to An Gearanach 'unnerving' for a few moves. The final four Munros I did with a light pack from Meanach bothy the next day.

Fourteen years passed before I returned, although I had never intended to leave it so long – other mountains and walks just ate up the time. This time I planned the walk rather more carefully. Firstly, I decided to walk from east to west as this means ascending the outlier of Sgurr Eilde Mor at the start of the walk. The best views are also to the west. More importantly, I decided to camp high the night before rather than do the whole round from Glen Nevis, although this did mean carrying camping gear. While I wanted to walk the whole ridge in a day, I also wanted to enjoy it.

So, late one July evening I walked up through the Glen Nevis gorge, that spectacular chasm of steep rock, wild forest, deep pools and crashing waterfalls that forms a barrier between the easily accessible lower glen and the mountain-ringed sanctuary of the upper glen, and then climbed the grassy slopes to the col between Binnein Beag and Binnein Mor where I found a fine campsite with magnificent views across Glen Nevis to Ben Nevis, Aonach Mor, Aonach Beag and the silvery Grey Corries. The next morning dawned fine. Thirty-six minutes saw me up and down Binnein Beag. A second breakfast, then I packed up camp and set off on the path that leads across the steep northern slopes of Binnein Mor to the broad col with Sgurr Eilde Mor. There is a fine lochan on the col, which is also the lowest point on the Mamores ridge. I left my pack and climbed the steep slopes of Sgurr Eilde Mor. Back at the col I headed up to the south top of Binnein Mor, where I again left my pack before climbing to the summit of this, the highest peak in the Mamores. It is a fine peak, the culmination of three narrow ridges, and gives excellent views west along the ridge.

Binnein Beag and Sgurr Eilde Mor both feel cut off from the rest of the ridge by Binnein Mor, and it was only on the summit of that peak that I really felt I was on a long ridge walk. The summits now came thick and fast, or so it seemed. The individual tops did not really matter in fact – it was the ridge as a whole and the rhythm of walking on and on, for hour after hour, high above the world and surrounded by superb mountains. The ridge to An Gearanach was definitely sharper and more exposed than the Devil's Ridge, but I could not see why it had been unnerving the first time. On the very top of Sgurr a'Mhaim a snow bunting was feeding two fledglings. Because Sgurr a'Mhaim is out on a spur it has

superb views of the rest of the Mamores and along the whole length of Glen Nevis. It is this peak that dominates the view from the road in lower Glen Nevis, sometimes being mistaken for Ben Nevis.

The walk was so enjoyable it felt effortless. I almost seemed to be flowing along. This feeling started to fade on the long, undulating section from

Looking west along the Mamores from Binnein Mor with Sgurr a'Mhaim dominating the view.

Stob Ban to the last, lowest and least interesting Munro, Mullach nan Coirean. Most of the ridge is made up of pale mica-schist and white quartzite but beyond Stob Ban this changes to red granite, a change that can be seen clearly. The best descent to Glen Nevis from Mullach nan Coirean is by the north-east ridge, my ascent route on my first attempt. Hoping to find water, as I was very thirsty after my successful complete traverse, I descended instead into Coire Riabhach. This was not a good idea. There was no water in the upper corrie and the lower corrie was very boggy. Logging roads led through the commercial forestry on the final descent to Glen Nevis. Lying in the tent that evening I wrote in my journal, 'What a long glorious day!'

BEN NEVIS AND THE CARN MOR DEARG ARETE

Ben Nevis was tremendous, curving from green to brown, then to dark cleaving crags reaching to jagged scars of red rock that thrust from dazzling snow edges.

Tom Weir, *Highland Days*

Start/finish:	Achintee Farm, Glen Nevis
Summits:	Carn Mor Dearg 1,223m (4,012ft), Ben Nevis 1,344m (4,406ft)
Distance:	16km (10 miles)
Navigation:	Moderate
Terrain:	Difficult
Winter:	Very difficult
Map:	Harveys 1:25,000 Superwalker: Ben Nevis. OS 1:25,000 Outdoor Leisure 32: Mountainmaster of Ben Nevis

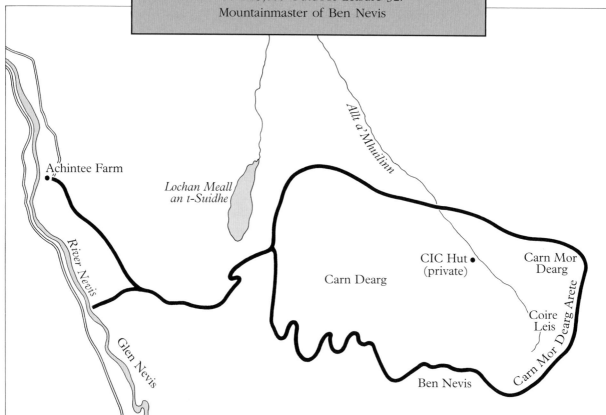

Ben Nevis is not only the highest mountain in Britain, it also has the biggest cliff, its awesome and complex north face being made up of huge rock walls and buttresses split by long gullies and dramatic ridges. This mountain wall is 3km (2 miles) long and reaches a maximum height of 610m (2,000ft). There are many hard rock and ice climbs but also scrambling lines for those walkers who wish to experience it at close quarters.

Linked to Ben Nevis by a graceful, curving arete is the tiny, pointed peak of Carn Mor Dearg. The contrast between the two peaks – one a solid bulk, the other an almost delicate cone – could not be greater. Carn Mor Dearg lies across Coire Leis from the north face and is a grand viewpoint for the cliffs.

That is when the weather is good, of course, which it rarely is on The Ben, as it is often familiarly known. Both the possible meanings of the full name refer to the conditions usually found here. The most popular theory is that the name derives from the Gaelic 'nimheil' or 'nibheis', meaning evil or venomous. Less generally accepted is that it comes from some variation on the old European word 'neb' meaning cloud or water.

The last would fit, as the mountain is certainly wet, with a mean annual rainfall of around 400cm (157in) and a maximum of 600cm (240in). Much of this falls as snow, as it is also a cold mountain, with a mean monthly temperature at the summit a third of a degree below freezing. An extra hundred metres or so of height and there would be glaciers. Cloud caps the summit most days of the year and there are an average of 261 gales a year. Given all this, I am quite surprised that on my half-dozen ascents the top has been clear three times. There have been

a few occasions when the weather has been so bad that I failed to reach the top, however, and a couple when I never set off at all.

The first known ascent was by botanist James Robertson in 1771 in order to collect plants for Edinburgh University. During the nineteenth century it became a popular tourist destination. Weather data was first collected in 1881 on behalf of the Scottish Meteorological Society by Clement Wragge of Fort William, who climbed to the summit every day during the summer of that year and again

On the Carn Mor Dearg arete.

during the summer and autumn of 1882, quite a feat considering that there was no path then and no shelter on the top. In 1883 the observatory, whose ruins can still be found near the summit cairn, was opened. This was staffed year round until its closure in 1904. It later reopened as part of the hotel that operated on the top until the 1918. At that time charges were made for using the pony track to the summit.

Also dating back to the nineteenth century is the Ben Nevis Race, which began in 1895. This is still held on the first Saturday of September. Astonishingly, the winning times are around 1 hour 45 minutes – and that's up *and* down.

Like most walkers, the runners use the old pony track that zigzags up the broad, stony north-west face. This Tourist Route, as it is usually called, is tedious, however, and best left for the descent. The ascent via Carn Mor Dearg and the arete is vastly superior: a splendid, scenic, exciting mountain walk that is never boring and often thrilling.

Both walks begin at the same place, Achintee in Glen Nevis, and follow the same wide path across the steep slopes of Meall an t-Suidhe to the broad saddle containing Lochan Meall an t-Suidhe. Just above this rather desolate stretch of water the routes split. The way to Carn Mor Dearg now contours round the northern slopes of Carn Dearg NW, the north-western top of Ben Nevis, and then descends below the northern end of the cliffs to the Allt a'Mhuillin, the last water until the walk is nearly over. Fill your bottles here!

East of the stream rise the steep, even slopes of Carn Mor Dearg. These can be ascended almost anywhere to the ridge just north of the summit. Throughout the ascent there are increasingly fine views back to the gigantic north face, giving plenty of

excuses to stop for rests. The summit is also a good place to sit and study the tremendous view. The tiny building you can see far below is the Charles Inglis Clark Hut built in 1929. It is owned by the Scottish Mountaineering Club and is a base for climbers.

The Carn Mor Dearg arete curves round the head of Coire Leis from the summit to the boulder-strewn eastern slopes of Ben Nevis. Although narrow, it is quite easy and only involves a little scrambling in places. The views of the cliffs are fantastic throughout. The lowest point is 1,060m (3,478ft) so there is quite a climb up to the top of Ben Nevis.

On the last occasion I did this round it was quite a shock to emerge on to the summit of The Ben, as there were crowds all over the plateau and yet on the arete we had seen only a handful of people. I was wearing sports sandals and heard several muttered comments of disapproval and astonishment from walkers who had slogged up the Tourist Path in heavy boots. I didn't mind – my feet had never felt better! The summit has been cleared of much of the junk that littered it and is now a much more pleasant place than it was in the 1970s and 1980s. The view is extensive, but everything is so far away that it is not very interesting. The best views are from the edge of the cliffs – take care here though! The finest prospect I have had from the top was in winter after a climb up an easy gully. We crossed the plateau as the sun set and the light out to the west was wonderful, while the snow all around shone pink in the last rays of the day.

The descent down the Tourist Path is easy, but hard on the feet. Much of the path has been renovated and now consists of a staircase of stone slabs. Footwear with good shock-absorbing properties will be appreciated here.

The summit of Ben Nevis in June.

Interest is provided by the people rather than the scenery. On my last descent hordes were sweating up the stony slopes: over-equipped walkers in big boots with big packs; under-equipped tourists with plastic carrier bags and shoulder bags, dangling cameras, bright shirts, sun hats and dark glasses; families with the children running all over the slopes and playing on the last remaining snow patches while their slower, rucksack-burdened parents attempted to keep them under control; mountain bikers pushing their rugged steeds – all intent on climbing Britain's highest peak. It is not the summit that is the best reason for going, though – it is the getting there. And the best way to do that is on the other side of the mountain.

ACROSS THE HIGH TOPS OF THE CAIRNGORMS

*The sense of our minuteness on these empty wastes
became acute. I felt a tiny speck swallowed up in an
environment incomprehensibly great, like the flicker of
earthly life amid the uncountable galaxies.
Here we knew what it felt to be alone, yet to feel distant
kinship with the gods.*

W.H Murray, *Mountaineering in Scotland*

Start/finish:	Glen Feshie to Cock Bridge
Summits:	Braeriach 1,295m (4,248ft), Cairn Toul 1,293m (4,241ft), Ben MacDui 1,309m (4,296ft), Beinn a'Bhuird 1,196m (3,924ft), Ben Avon 1,171m (3,843ft)
Distance:	70km (43 miles)
Navigation:	Very difficult
Terrain:	Moderate
Winter:	Difficult
Maps:	OS 1:50,000 Sheets 36 and 37: Grantown and Cairngorm & Strathdon

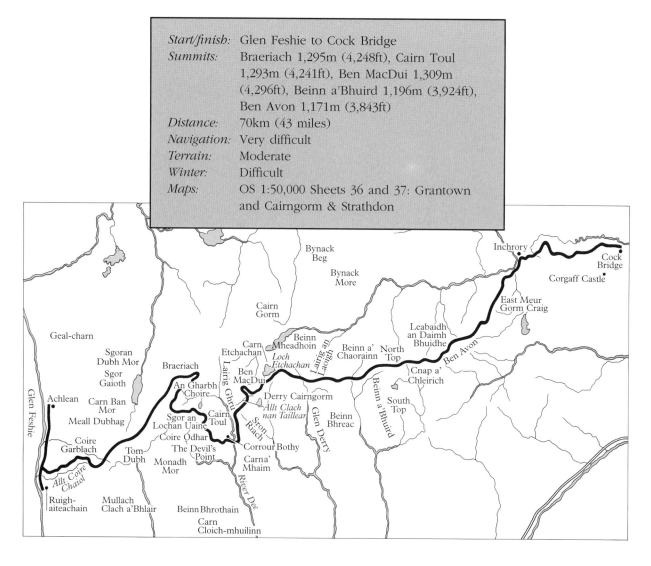

*On the ascent of
Cairn Toul.*

The largest area of high ground in the Highlands, in Britain in fact – a vast 1,000sq km (385sq mls) – lies between Glen Feshie and the Lecht road. Five of Scotland's ten highest peaks are here, along with 12 other Munros and a welter of tops. This is granite country, a land of high, bare plateaux and deep, cliff-rimmed corries fringed by some of the largest remnants of the old Caledonian forest. The scenery is spectacular, the sense of space overwhelming, the scope for walking enormous. In 1977 Cairn Gorm and Ben MacDui were the first Scottish hills I ever climbed, and the area is still one of my favourites.

For a straight-line distance of 45km (28 miles) west to east the Cairngorms are unbroken by roads. Three huge plateaux make up the area, split by the two passes of the Lairig Ghru and the Lairig an Laoigh. Although I had walked, skied and camped throughout the Cairngorms many times and had climbed all the peaks at least twice, it

was 14 years after my first visit before I crossed the region west to east in one journey. The six highest peaks have all been climbed in a single day both on foot and on ski, but as I was not intent on a fast crossing but rather wanted to savour the wildness and solitude of the region, I planned a 2½-day traverse. I also went in December, not the best time for doing long distances every day, but a month when meeting many other people on these popular tops was unlikely. The weather was a factor too, the region recording the highest wind-speeds in Britain. In a blizzard the crossing would be impossible. I went when high pressure was forecast for the next few days. There might be mist and heavy frosts and it would be cold, but there should not be high winds or rain or snow.

To ensure a dawn start, I was dropped at the road end at Achlean in Glen Feshie late one evening by a friend who would pick me up at Cock Bridge south of the Lecht at 1pm in

*Loch Avon from
the Cairngorm
plateau.*

three days' time if all went well. A chill southerly wind blew down the glen as I set off on the 5km (3 mile) walk south along the banks of the river Feshie to Ruigh-aiteachain, a spacious bothy set deep in the imposing Scots-pine forest that dominates the heart of the glen. A few stars could be seen, but the sky was mostly cloudy and I needed my headlamp to pick out the path.

The bothy was empty and cold, the thermometer reading just 2°C (36°F). There was plenty of wood drying inside so I lit a fire to take the chill off the air. Most of the heat vanished up the chimney, however, the temperature rising by just one meagre degree. The fire was cheerful though, and I could feel some warmth by huddling close to it. The bothy boasted a sofa and three armchairs, new additions since my last visit: the normal seats are well-polished pine logs.

By 11pm I was fast asleep in the wood-floored attic, warm and snug in my sleeping bag. The banging of the outer door and the sound of voices woke me at half-past midnight. Six people came in: three men, two women and a child aged around eight or nine it seemed from the voices. I could hear a dog pattering about too. Footsteps sounded on the wooden steps and a torch flashed. 'Someone asleep up here,' a voice said softly. The new arrivals were not particularly noisy, but they were directly below me and I could hear every word. A pressure stove roaring into life ensured I would not get any sleep until they went to bed. This was at 2am.

At 6.15am my alarm woke me. I lit a candle and crept downstairs. The cushioned seats of the chairs and sofa had been spread out on the floor as bedding for two dogs, an Alsatian and a large mongrel that looked to be mostly labrador. At my appearance they started to stretch and whimper. Their owner, asleep in a red sleeping bag next to them, stirred. 'They won't hurt you, don't mind them,' he murmured groggily, before slumping back to sleep. By the fire stood two pairs of wet boots, while a pair of child's damp tracksuit trousers hung from a drying line. Someone had had problems crossing the streams that have to be forded to reach the bothy. I tiptoed round the dogs to the table and lit my stove. The roar shattered the silence. It wasn't as noisy as the stove the others had but, despite being called the Whisperlite, it could not be described as quiet. After a hasty breakfast I packed up in the half dark.

As the day came greyly and slowly to life I set off up the ugly bulldozed track that leads up Coire Caol to the flat, almost featureless expanse of the Moine Mhor, or Great Moss. Waves of low cloud were rolling in from the south and the wind was bitterly cold. The ground was white with frost and every stream and pool was frozen solid. Warm sunshine bathed the pointed peak of Sgor Gaioth to the north and occasionally appeared through the clouds to the south. Mostly, though, I walked in mist on easterly compass bearings. I came out of the clouds on the southern slopes of mighty Braeriach, third highest in Scotland. A walker passed me near the summit, the only person I was to see on the tops all day. There was no more than a smattering of snow around the summit cairn. I have been here in May when it lay several feet deep with great curling cornices hanging over the steep drops above An Garbh Choire.

Braeriach lies at the northern end of one of the most superb high-level walks in the British hills. This runs for 5km (3 miles) round the edge of An Garbh Choire, a massive bowl carved out of the plateau and backed by high cliffs, to Cairn Toul, the fourth-highest Munro. From Braeriach's summit the corrie edge appeared to be a huge dam holding back the mass of cloud shrouding the Moine Mhor. To the east all was clear, with Ben MacDui shining in the sunlight above the deep cleft of the Lairig Ghru. At the lowest point between Braeriach and Cairn Toul, where the infant river Dee trickles over the cliffs from its source – the highest spring in Scotland at 1,190m (3,901ft) – not far away on the Moine Mhor the clouds broke over the corrie edge and dissipated themselves in the cauldron below. I dipped in and out of the mist as I followed the top of the cliffs. A few sizable patches of snow, the remnants of a big fall in November, and the icy bubbles of frozen overflows from the many streams made the going tricky in places. From the steep slopes of the fine sharp peak of Sgorr an Lochain Uaine I could see the lochan itself, nestled against the great cliffs below, and look back across An Garbh Coire to Braeriach. This summit is probably the best viewpoint of the walk, although it is clearly only a subsidiary of Cairn Toul which lies not far to the south-east.

The mist lapped Cairn Toul, giving views east to Ben MacDui but none back west. Where Braeriach is a great bear of a mountain, bulky and sprawling, Cairn Toul, the Hill of the Barn, is precise and neat with steep slopes and a clearly defined summit. Dropping down to the col with the next peak, The Devil's Point, I scanned the slopes ahead anxiously. My concern was that the initially steep descent into Coire Odhar, from where I would drop down into the Lairig Ghru, would be blocked by snow, as it had been the last time I had descended this way on a TGO Challenge coast-to-coast crossing of the

Highlands one May. Then my companion and I had had ice axes. Even so, we had had to traverse out across the corrie headwall and cut some steps in the icy old snow before we got down safely. With no axe, that option was not open to me. If I could not gain the corrie directly I would turn south-west and descend the gentler slopes into Glen Geusachan, which leads east to the river Dee. As it was, the descent path was clear of snow – just. Large rock-hard patches lay to either side and the stony path was icy and treacherous, but I was able to descend relatively easily with the support of my staff.

As I reached easier ground I saw two walkers heading for Corrour Bothy, which lay directly below. Remembering the disturbance of the night before, I passed the bothy by and headed for the river, to camp on a good site just by

the confluence of the Allt a'Choire Odhair and the Dee. I felt tired, having walked 30km (19 miles) and ascended 1,550m (5,000ft) with a 20kg (44lb) pack in 7 hours, and felt I was more likely to get a good night's sleep in the solitude of the tent. I am not happy about using this bothy anymore, anyway.

Corrour is a tiny, one-roomed stone bothy nestling under the great shining slabs of The Devil's Point, across the river Dee from the steep broken slopes of Carn a'Mhaim. It is a fine, grand spot, redolent of all that is most dramatic and awe inspiring in the hills. Unlike more recent intrusions, Corrour, built as a gamekeeper's hut in 1877, fits well into these surroundings, its rough-hewn, speckled-granite walls looking almost as natural as the heather and the peat. Since the end of World War I many

The Lairig Ghru pass in August.

walkers and climbers have found shelter, sanctuary even, in its bare confines. Yet, despite the many memorable visits I have made to Corrour, whether on skis in the crisp delight of a bright winter's day or after a summer slog through driving rain, recent visits have left me with an uneasy feeling, with thoughts that at first I did not want to explore, that I tried to suppress.

These half-formulated ideas nagged away at me until I worked through them and realized what I was trying to ignore. Despite my love of the place and the memories it holds for me, I feel that Corrour should be closed, perhaps even pulled down, and the reasons I came to this sad conclusion undoubtedly apply elsewhere and relate to the whole question of how we use and abuse our mountains and wild places.

Alone in Corrour a few years before the Cairngorm crossing, I had sat reading the bothy journal by candlelight

Sunset over the Cairngorms.

while from outside there came the elemental sounds of the rain and the wind and the distant roaring of rutting stags. For years one of the pleasures in staying in bothies has been to see who else has been there and what they have done, to pick up hints for routes and to read the thoughts and stories of people who I will never meet but with whom I share a love of the hills. The Corrour bothy book was not a joy to read, however. Instead it left me feeling quite disturbed, for among the entries from those who came there by choice and with respect were many, far too many, from those who were only there under duress, dragged there by some organization or other because it was meant to be 'good for them' or 'character building' or some such flimsy justification. Their entries showed despair and disgust, some of them hatred. It saddens me greatly to think that the hills are under pressure in part from people who do not even want to be there.

People who hate a place are hardly going to treat it with care. In a boulder field behind Corrour the artificial sheen of plastic bags full of half-rotted rubbish peeps out from under many of the rocks, while the sordid pink strands of used toilet paper straggle out from beneath many more. It is a depressing place, and one that I have felt quite ashamed of when there with others.

The Lairig Ghru is a very popular walk. In places the wide, muddy scar of the main track is worn and eroded while at some points the side path leading to Corrour is a quagmire. Few of those who come through the pass fail to visit the bothy. Indeed, the bothy book shows that the place is frequently overcrowded and always packed throughout the summer. It also reveals that many only walk the Lairig Ghru because the bothy is there. From their

own words, many are people who would not come this way without shelter being provided for them, who would think twice if they had to camp.

The closure of Corrour would in my view greatly lessen the growing pressure on the Lairig Ghru and the remote fastnesses of the Cairngorms. Its very existence makes access easier and safer and encourages visitation. That it has been there since the last century and has sheltered walkers for decades is not a reason to keep it.

On the north side of the Lairig Ghru there used to be another shelter, an ugly concrete blockhouse built in 1957 as a memorial to Lt Col Angus Sinclair, who died in a winter accident in the Cairngorms. The Sinclair Hut was dismantled in 1991 because of problems with erosion, litter and graffiti. Although in favour of its removal, I can see that it has increased the pressure on Corrour. If Corrour were also to go, people would have to camp, which would discourage some and also spread out the impact instead of concentrating it at one spot. Some of the rubbish that disfigures the area around Corrour would probably not be carried in if the people had to lug tents as well. (In case anyone thinks I am being hypocritical, I always carry a tent.)

Corrour is not, I'm afraid, an isolated case. There are other popular bothies in sensitive areas whose continued use should be questioned. I love bothies and the idea of bothies. But I think we have to face up to the reality of what providing shelter in certain areas is doing to the hills, and ask whether it would be better to forego the comforts of a solid roof and a dry floor in order to help preserve the wildness and splendour of the mountains.

A gusty, southerly wind rattled the tent occasionally, but I left the doors open so that I could lie back and admire the beautiful starry sky. The temperature was -5°C (23°F). At 5am the cold shock of raindrops on my face woke me. I looked out. The hills were clear of cloud despite the heavy rain. By the time I set off the rain had stopped and the clouds were starting to disintegrate. A short way north on the Lairig Ghru path took me to the less distinct path that climbs beside the Allt Clach nan Taillear. Fine views back to the white, sparkling, twisting line of the river Dee between Carn a'Mhaim and The Devil's Point, twin sentinels guarding the southern approach to the Lairig Ghru and the magic heartland of the Cairngorms, give many excuses to stop on this steep ascent.

Eventually I left the stream and the path for the boulder-strewn rounded spur to the north that leads directly to the summit of Ben MacDui, second-highest peak in Britain and a huge, sprawling, magnificent mountain. The view across the Lairig Ghru to Cairn Toul and Braeriach and the great scoop of An Garbh Choire is superb, although the best place to see it from is a few hundred metres west of the trig point. A cold wind blew across the stony wastes of the broad, rounded summit and I cowered behind one of the myriad shelter walls for a snack. Across the plateau 5km (3 miles) to the north-east lay the rounded dome of Cairn Gorm. I considered an ascent as it is one of the six highest tops in the Cairngorms and I liked the idea of climbing them all in one walk. However, I wanted even more to maintain the wilderness feel of the walk and Cairn Gorm, sadly, is sullied on its north side by the ugly intrusion of the ski resort. Anathema to lovers of the freedom of the hills, a wide fenced-in path leads from the highest chairlift to the summit. I decided against an ascent. Five truly wild mountains would do. I would head east.

From the top I picked a way from rock to rock among the patches of snow and ice to the path leading down to Loch Etchachan. A heavily laden party of four passed me labouring up, their bulging packs half-hidden under ropes and ice axes, their feet encased in rigid plastic mountaineering boots. The last of the four grunted a greeting and glanced with disapproval at my lightweight footwear and thin trousers. I tramped on down, making endless little diversions to avoid the frozen streams and icy patches that made up the path in places.

Loch Etchachan was almost completely frozen over and looked grim and cold. From the loch the path continues down Coire Etchachan, the dark and impressive cliff of Creagan a'Choire Etchachan dominating the view. Where the path starts to turn south (it descends to Derry Lodge) I left it, crossed upper Glen Derry and then went straight up a steep but shallow, grassy gully to the Moine Bhealaidh, a flat expanse of peat hags and small lochans lying between the two Munros of Beinn a'Chaorainn and Beinn Bhreac. The bogs were frozen solid, which made them hard underfoot but easier to cross than they would be in wet weather.

On my last two visits the moss had been snow covered and I had been on skis, and I noticed how much longer it took to cross these wide-open spaces on foot. At least it was clear. On one ski trip I had climbed Beinn a'Chaorainn in thick mist, only to discover I had forgotten my compass. The next few hours were a salutary lesson in why one is necessary, as I tried to stay on a straight line south to Beinn Bhreac. This proved impossible and I went round in circles, crossing my own tracks several times and once reclimbing Beinn a'Chaorainn and starting again.

The River Feshie in autumn.

Eventually I left marks where my tracks crossed so that I could see which way I had gone the last time I had passed each junction! Finally abandoning my southward journey, I had a rather exciting descent down the Glas Allt Mor, whose ravine is quite narrow and steep in places, to the Lairig an Laoigh path.

This time the sky was clear and I was able to enjoy the excellent and comprehensive view of the central Cairngorms, which reached from Bynack More in the north, round over Cairn Gorm and Cairn Lochain to Ben MacDui, on either side of which stood the summits of Braeriach and Cairn Toul. South of the last lay Monadh Mor, Beinn Bhrotain and the cone of Carn Cloich-mhuilinn, planned as his last Munro by Sir Hugh himself and one of the only three he never climbed, but now demoted from the Tables on the grounds of insignificance although some, myself included, feel it should have been retained for historical reasons.

Just across Glen Derry, Beinn Mheadhoin and Derry Cairngorm took up their subservient positions as satellites of Ben MacDui. Overall, this western side of the easternmost of the three great Cairngorm plateaux is the best place to see the complexities of the highest tops. From here Ben MacDui's dominance is obvious, all the other peaks belonging to it.

Turning east, I slowly climbed the long, gentle slopes of Beinn a'Bhuird to the North Top, the highest point on the 3km (1¾ miles) long ridge of Scotland's 'table mountain'. The sky to the south had glowed red under the clouds all day but the colour was now deepening over distant Beinn A'Ghlo, reminding me that the day was ending and I needed a campsite. I had last been here ten months earlier on a ski tour and

I seemed to remember some flat ground just south of The Sneck, the narrow gap between Beinn a'Bhuird and Ben Avon, the easternmost of the high tops. From the minor top of Cnap a'Chleirich, I looked back to see a superb sunset over the dark snow-splashed cliffs of the great eastern corries of Beinn a'Bhuird.

My memory was accurate and I was soon pitching the tent just below The Sneck at a height of 950m (3,100ft). The streams running over the rock slabs above my camp were frozen into sheets of rippling white ice, but just below the stream was flowing between banks of snow. The temperature was -2°C (28°F) and the sky was clear and packed with stars.

By dawn a gusty south wind had brought high clouds, although a red glow to the south showed that the sun was there somewhere. For a few brief seconds it split the clouds, to light up the snow on the slopes to the west with a warm pink glow. Ben Avon lies just above the Sneck to the east and I was on top 35 minutes after breaking camp. A short scramble leads to the top of the summit tor, the highest of the many strange granite excrescences that dot this massive mountain. I gazed back over the hills I had climbed. It had been a good walk, but it was coming to an end.

I descended over the stony plateau past East Meur Gorm Craig to pick up the stalker's path that runs between Clach Bhan and Meall Gaineimh, a complex route that could prove tricky in poor visibility. Once the path was gained it was an easy, quick descent to the right-angled bend in the river Avon at Inchrory. From here a bulldozed road leads east through pleasant woodland to the river Don and the stark ruins of Corgaff Castle at Cock Bridge. I arrived at 1.30pm.

GLEN FINNAN

SGURR THUILM AND SGURR NAN COIREACHAN

Bulky big brutes.

Hamish Brown, *Hamish's Mountain Walk*

Start/finish:	Glenfinnan, on the A830 Fort William–Mallaig road
Summits:	Sgurr Thuilm 963m (3,159ft), Sgurr nan Coireachan 956m (3,136ft)
Distance:	21km (13 miles)
Navigation:	Difficult
Terrain:	Difficult
Winter:	Difficult
Map:	OS 1:50,000 Sheet 40: Loch Shiel

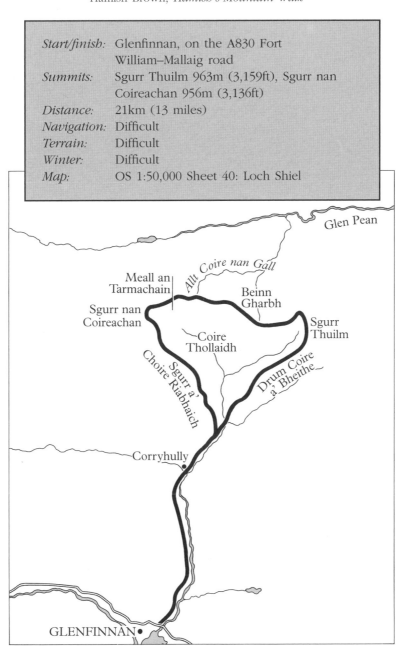

The journey from Fort William to Mallaig, whether by rail or road, is one of the most spectacular in Britain. Here the passive traveller can gain at least a slight sense of the glories of the hills. Although even the lower peaks of the area are well worth climbing, there is one outstanding walk that can be done in a day from the road or railway: the Glen Finnan Horseshoe. This takes you to the southern edges of the vast wild lands known as the Rough Bounds of Knoydart, over terrain rugged enough to also give a taste of what lies further north and deeper into the mountains.

Soon after the land begins to rise and crowd in upon the road and railway, the head of Loch Shiel and the tiny hamlet of Glenfinnan are reached. Near here Bonnie Prince Charlie raised his Standard in 1745 at the start of his doomed campaign to take the British throne. A monument built to commemorate this event stands at the head of the loch, though apparently it actually took place on a nearby hilltop. The lochside is a more dramatic and accessible spot, however! The monument is now in the care of the NTS and there is a visitor centre and café here where, among other items, you can buy a map if you have left yours behind or, as happened to me on one very wet backpacking trip through the area, if the pocket of your waterproof jacket has failed to keep it dry.

There is a station at Glenfinnan and an NTS car park. Vehicles can also be left on rough ground near the start of the track up Glen Finnan on the west side of the bridge over the River Finnan. This is where the walk starts, initially following this track to the splendid Glenfinnan Railway Viaduct, built in 1899 and one of the first such structures. There is a story that one of the hollow pillars holds the remains of a horse and cart that fell into it

during its construction. Through one of the arches the tiny rounded summit of Sgurr Thuilm can be seen.

Beyond the viaduct a Landrover track winds up the glen, past the rushing, sparkling waters of the river, its banks dotted with clumps of birch, willow and alder. In spring and early summer the marshy meadows are dotted with flowers and sandpipers can be seen bobbing on the stones at the water's edge, while cuckoos call from the trees.

To either side rugged hillsides rise upwards in a series of broken crags and steep heathery slopes, a grand scene marred only by the sight of Glenfinnan Lodge to the north, an ugly suburban block of a building that is totally out of keeping with the surroundings. Below the lodge lies Corryhully bothy, an open refuge maintained by the estate and featuring the luxury of electric lights. This would make a good base and could be used if you wanted to spread the walk over two days or climb some of the other hills that rise above the glen, Streap to the north-east being a particularly worthwhile objective. I was once very grateful for the shelter of Corryhully on a TGO Challenge coast-to-coast walk after crossing 796m (2,610ft) Sgurr an Utha to the west in rapidly deteriorating weather. I had descended in lashing rain and a blasting wind, to arrive at the bothy drenched and tired and very glad not to have to camp for the night.

On a more recent visit, however, my companion and I were glad to camp as the weather was superb. Who wants to be enclosed in a dark, dank bothy when the sun is shining? Instead we went on up the glen a little way to camp in the mouth of Coire Thollaidh, which is encircled by the ridges of Sgurr Thuilm and Sgurr nan Coireachan. If you have a spare hour or so a walk up

Opposite: *Looking up Coire Thollaidh to Sgurr nan Coireachan.*

this coire is an enjoyable way to spend it, as the stream tumbles down a series of small cascades in miniature gorges overhung with ferns and flowers, while above rise the rocky slopes of the hills, the most impressive crags being high above to the west below the south-east ridge of Sgurr nan Coireachan.

Whether you are camping, staying in the bothy or doing the walk in a day, the entrance to Coire Thollaidh is where you leave the track up the glen for the mountainside. The round can be done in either direction, but I would recommend going east to west as this gives the best views as you head towards Loch Morar and the sea. Sgurr nan Coireachan, although slightly lower, is also much the finer summit of the two. It would be an anti-climax to do Sgurr Thuilm last. Whichever way you go, attention needs to be paid to navigation. There are traces of paths throughout the route, but none of these should be relied upon as they are easily lost and some do not take the best line.

The route starts by heading north-west up the initially steep grassy slopes of Drum Coire a'Bheithe, a long ridge that leads directly to the summit of Sgurr Thuilm. The summit itself is slightly north of the main ridge, so you have to go out and back to it. From the top, the ridge out to Sgurr nan Coireachan can be seen twisting away to the west with the dark slash of Loch Morar beyond it, while to the north, in Knoydart, a dense confusing mass of steep-sided peaks and deep glens fades away into the horizon – an inspiring view to those, like me, who love the idea of mountains without end. Eastwards the view is more open with gentler, mostly lower, hills sweeping away to the great bulk, snow-splashed most of the year, of Ben Nevis. Mirroring the Knoydart hills to the south is the equally impressive tangle of the

peaks of Moidart and Ardgour, not quite so high but just as rough.

The walking, so far fairly straightforward, becomes much more interesting beyond Sgurr Thuilm as the ridge, narrow enough to give the feeling of being high above the corries that abut it, but not so narrow as to give any difficulties or feelings of exposure, bobs and dips over the tops of Beinn Gharbh and Meall an Tarmachain. There is much bare rock, and several outcrops offer optional scrambles. A line of rusted fence posts runs along the crest, a useful navigational aid in mist but the mountains would be better without the intrusion. While the views to the north continually draw the eye, gradually opening up to the west is the jagged line of the coast. Immediately to the north, wild remote Coire Dhuibh and Coire nan Gall cut deeply into the hillside.

Little visited, these corries can give adventures of their own, as I found one February when two of us climbed Sgurr Thuilm from Glen Pean to the north by way of Coire Dhuibh. As we traversed upwards out of the coire towards the ridge, the cold swirling winter mists began to clear and we became aware that the ground was steepening and the hard and icy snow under our feet hung over a dark nothingness. The corrie floor suddenly seemed a long way below us. Caution took over and, ice axes in hand, we chose our route more carefully, picking a way over frozen grass and iced rocks to the ridge. Stinging spindrift was blasting over the summit and it was bitterly cold, so we did not linger but were soon heading down the peak's north ridge.

The final climb to Sgurr nan Coireachan can be exciting too, as I found in the middle of May one year when slopes of old, hard snow had to be ascended, a tricky business when we had no ice axes, just trekking poles. The summit is small and rocky and care may be needed in finding the way off. The first time I came here I raced a rolling wave of cloud that was pouring in from the sea and flooding up the glens and over the lower hills, almost running along the ridge from Sgurr Thuilm despite my heavy pack. We reached the summit at the same time, the vista fading as the summit cairn came into view. Compass bearings and careful route-finding took me down the rock terraces and through the outcrops of the steep, broken northern slopes of the mountain to the narrow notch of Glen Pean. The hardest section was at the bottom where, as I wrote in my journal, I had a 'time-consuming scrabble around innumerable tree-girt crags'.

For those returning to Glenfinnan the way is somewhat easier, although care is still needed, especially in mist or when snow lies on the ground, as sections of the south-east ridge of Sgurr nan Coireachan are very steep and there are many crags. The way to Sgurr a'Choire Riabhaich is rough but easy, as long as you take care not to tumble over the rock terraces that lie across the broad ridge. Beyond that top, however, the ground steepens appreciably. Traces of paths abound, but I would ignore those that leave the ridge and stick to the crest. It is more direct and no steeper than the alternatives, some of which are very loose and slippery, as I know after being lured down one of them on the west side of the ridge on one occasion. A good stalker's path climbs up the east side of the ridge at its lower end. This is worth aiming for to make the last section of the descent easier. Once you are down, there just remains the walk out along the glen to complete a magnificent mountain day.

SGURR NA CICHE AND GARBH CIOCH MHOR

A melee of contorted outcrops destroying all directional awareness and enforcing many a scrambling detour.

Martin Moran, The Munros in Winter

Start/finish:	Strathan, at the west end of Loch Arkaig
Summits:	Sgurr nan Coireachan 953m (3,125ft), Garbh Chioch Mhor 1,026m (3,365ft), Sgurr na Ciche 1,040m (3,410ft)
Distance:	21km (13 miles) round trip from Strathan, 8km (5 miles) from Glen Dessary to Loch Nevis
Navigation:	Difficult
Terrain:	Difficult
Winter:	Difficult
Map:	OS 1:50,000 Sheet 33: Loch Alsh & Glen Shiel

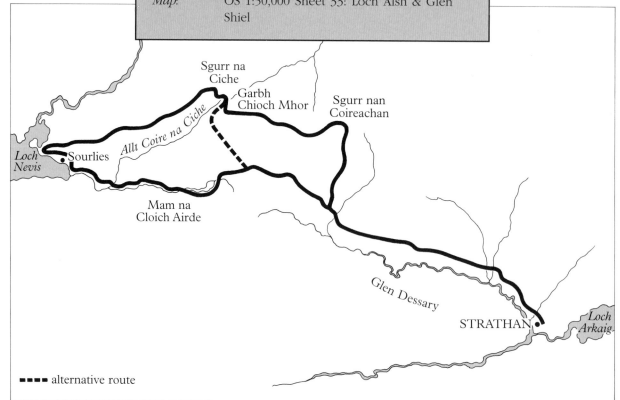

■■■ alternative route

At the end of the interminable winding, single-track road along Loch Arkaig lies Glen Dessary, a once inhabited but now empty glen, dark with dense plantations of spruce. The north side of the glen is dominated by the ridge running from Sgurr nan Coireachan over Garbh Chioch Mhor to Sgurr na Ciche, one of the finest in the Highlands – a rugged, sinuous, rocky crest that is always interesting and often challenging. The western end overlooks Loch Nevis and is far from Loch Arkaig, making the traverse of the ridge and the return to the start point in a day a lengthy venture. Too lengthy in my view, and I have always camped at either end of the ridge or else used the two bothies that lie in the area. These are small, however, and popular in summer. Overall, I would recommend camping, as there are many excellent sites.

The first two times I walked the ridge the clouds were down and the views minimal. On the second occasion there was much snow on the crest, even though it was mid-May, making for an exciting traverse, especially as we had no ice axes or crampons. On my next visit, the first in an east-west direction, the cliché of third time lucky came true, the sun shone and the air was clear of the haze of humidity that often bedevils the hills when it is not raining.

From the upper western end of Glen Dessary a long, steep 732m (2,400ft) pathless climb up rough slopes leads to the summit of Sgurr nan Coireachan. This is hard work and tiresome, especially with a full pack, but it does get you high quickly. On my third visit we were greeted with a vast panorama of the Scottish mountains and much time was spent trying to identify various peaks. One was unmistakable: the massive snow-striped bulk of Ben Nevis away to the south-east. A bitter wind was blowing from the north and with it came clouds and occasional flurries of snow, belying the fact that it was July. This mixed weather continued throughout the day. One minute we

Sgurr na Ciche from Loch Nevis.

were walking in bright sunshine, sweltering in our rain jackets, the next we were cowering under our hoods as stinging snow whipped our faces. Between the squalls the air had an amazing clarity, with the sky a deep blue and the distant views sharp in a way unusual in Scotland. Closer to hand the rocks glittered with mica chips, and the grass shone green with spring growth and white with the latest spattering of snow. Some of the showers passed us by and we watched as grey curtains blotted out nearby hills or swept over The Ben.

The route now heads westwards along broad, rugged slopes to Garbh Chioch Mhor. A wall runs along this twisting ridge, useful for navigation in poor visibility. In clear weather following the ridge is not difficult, and you can admire the broken crags and great rock walls that abut this fine mountain, promoted to Munro status in the revision of 1981. As we travelled towards the distinctive steeply pointed pyramid of Sgurr na Ciche, the magic of Knoydart captured me again. Where else, I thought, could anyone possibly want to be?

The wall continues as far as the gap of Feadan na Ciche, beyond which

Loch Nevis from the slopes of Sgurr na Ciche.

grassy ramps lead between large rock outcrops to the summit of Sgurr na Ciche. As we made this ascent, two parties passed us heading the other way. One pair with daypacks asked where we were heading after Sgurr na Ciche. 'Straight down the ridge to Loch Nevis,' I replied. 'With those packs?' they said, eyeing our full backpacks with surprise. 'I wouldn't advise it,' one went on, 'it's very steep and there are some rocks you'll have to climb down.' Instead, he suggested we return to the col with Garbh Chioch Mhor and descend into Coire na Ciche (the best way down if you are returning to Loch

Arkaig the same day – when a terrace is reached at around 650m (2,130ft) this can be followed to the top of the Mam na Cloich Airde, the low pass at the head of Glen Dessary). As we continued along the ridge I thought hard about what they had said but could remember no problems with the ridge, which I had used on my two previous ascents of Sgurr na Ciche.

The remains of a couple of decaying tri points decorate (litter is perhaps a better word) the summit of Sgurr na Ciche, but there is more to attract the attention – much more, as in clear weather this is a superlative viewpoint for the Knoydart peaks, the islands that lie off the coast and, directly below, Loch Nevis, a tremendous scene of wild grandeur.

The descent ridge is very steep at the top and does have a couple of short bits of easy scrambling, but nothing that is a problem. Heading up, the pair we had met on the ridge had probably taken some of the small crags direct – fun to do when carrying just a daysack – and not realized there were easier ways. We had more difficulty threading a way through the lower crags immediately above blue-green Loch Nevis and the dark smudge of Sourlies bothy. A tent on the green sward by the beach, a fine camping spot, showed that, as usual, there were people here.

Disappointingly, there were red paint daubs on the rocks all the way down the ridge, an unsightly and unnecessary addition to the scene, and worse than cairns because much less easy to obliterate. I cursed the vandals who had desecrated this mountainside, calling on the gods of the wild to condemn them to wander for eternity lost in a dense mist.

From Loch Nevis a good path leads east over the Mam na Cloich Airde and back down into Glen Dessary.

LIATHACH

*One felt that Liathach was alive, ever alert to pounce
upon any mistake.*

Lea MacNally, *Torridon*

Start/finish:	Torridon NTS visitor centre
Summits:	Spidean a'Chore Leith 1,054m (3,456ft) and Mullach an Rathain 1,023m (3,358ft) are the two Munros. Am Fasarinen 927m (3,050ft) is also traversed, while options are Bidean Toll a'Mhuic 975m (3,200ft), Stuc a'Choire Dhuibh Bhig 913m (2,995ft) and Meall Dearg 960m (3,150ft)
Distance:	10km (6 miles)
Navigation:	Difficult
Terrain:	Difficult
Winter:	Very difficult
Map:	OS 1:25,000 Outdoor Leisure 8: The Cuillin & Torridon Hills

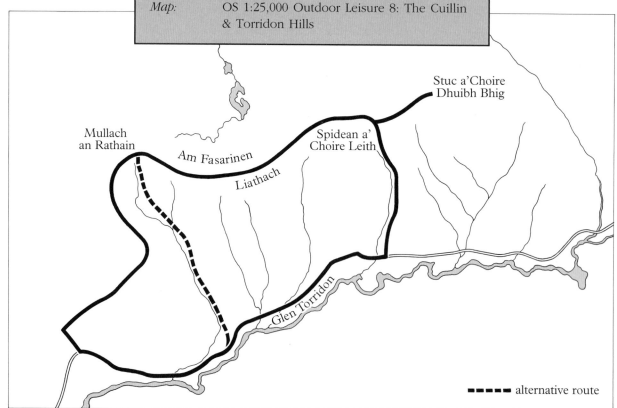

- - - - - alternative route

*Liathach at dusk,
from Loch an
Eion.*

Liathach, the Grey One, dominates Glen Torridon. Its split castellated ramparts soar above the road, drawing the eye upwards. However, although impressive, the mountain is too close to be seen properly when approached this way. To see Liathach in all its glory requires distance. The classic viewpoint is from Loch Clair to the east; even better, to my mind, is the astounding view from the south, especially if you have walked from Achnashellach. This is how I first came to Liathach, to be overwhelmed by the sudden appearance of a vast, gully-seamed wall topped by a jagged crest rising to a shining white summit pyramid as I descended past Loch an Eion towards Loch Torridon. This view makes it clear that Liathach is not a single peak but a ridge of mountains with a single name. It is in fact 8km (5 miles) long and there are seven separate summits.

There are several regularly used routes up Liathach, and confident scramblers could find many more. The standard route climbs beside the Allt an Doire Ghairbh near the eastern end of the mountain into Toll a'Meitheach, and then to a low point on the main ridge east of Spidean a'Choire Leith, the highest summit on Liathach. Although steep, this is not a difficult ascent.

Most advice says that the best way to traverse Liathach is from east to west, mainly for the views this gives. My preference, however, is for west to east, ascending the westernmost top Mullach an Rathain first, as Spidean is clearly the finest as well as the highest of Liathach's five main tops and I would rather have it as the climax of the day. Also, the hardest part of the walk – the scramble along the Am Fasarinen pinnacles – lies west of the summit and it seems to me perverse to climb the peak first and then undertake the most difficult section. Having walked the ridge in both directions, I would definitely recommend crossing Am Fasarinen before climbing Spidean a'Choire Leith, as this approach makes

*Am Fasarinen and
Mullach an
Rathain, Liathach.*

reaching the summit much more
satisfying.

There are several possible routes up
to the ridge at the west end. The easiest
starts close to the clump of pines about
1km (⅔ml) east of the NTS information
centre and campsite at the Torridon
road junction and follows the Allt an
Tuill Bhain.

A more exciting, though more
arduous, climb starts directly behind the
campsite. High up, a narrow ridge can
be seen running up to Mullach an
Rathain. The very top of this ridge starts
off in a south-westerly direction down
gentle slopes from Mullach an Rathain,
before narrowing into a series of small
pinnacles below which it broadens and
is dotted with rock buttresses, before
losing its identity just above the glen
floor. This ridge does not stand out on
the OS Outdoor Leisure map, close

study being required to locate it among
the mass of contours and features. I
found it by studying the mountainside
from below looking for a way up, not
from the map.

Any day spent on Liathach would be
worthwhile whatever the weather, but a
view is always memorable. I was
certainly pleased to have dry, sunny
weather when I first climbed this
southern face of Mullach an Rathain,
especially as on both my previous
ascents of Liathach the cloud had been
firmly clamped round the summits.
A sunny day does have disadvantages,
however, as you will soon get hot and
sweaty. Liathach is steep everywhere,
one of those hills where kilometres
mean nothing. Three-quarters of a
kilometre of floundering through deep
heather boulder fields and steep, loose
quartzite scree, while climbing well over

1,050m (3,500ft) is far more tiring than walking 8km (5 miles) or more over easier terrain.

There is no path to the ridge leading to Mullach an Rathain – you simply aim for its broad base, meandering through the thick vegetation and occasional bogs and round the many boulders that bar the way. The base of the ridge being indistinct, you find yourself on it rather than reach it, the slopes falling away on either side signalling where you are. Buttresses of warm, red-gold Torridonian sandstone are scattered over the lower section. These can be climbed or avoided, although going over them is more exciting. The rough crystalline rock provides good friction and nowhere is the climbing difficult.

These broken buttresses continue to about 150m (500ft) below the main ridge. Here the ridge narrows abruptly and becomes a series of little pinnacles that give interesting and slightly exposed scrambling, although none of the pitches is very long. These pinnacles could be avoided by a traverse below them on steep grass to the east, but this seemed to me when I crossed a small section of it to see what it was like to be less pleasant than the rocky crest, which at least has positive handholds. In the wet I imagine that the ridge would prove much safer too, as it would under snow, but of course then the ascent would be much more serious.

All too soon, however, the scramble is over and a narrow, stony but gentle slope leads to Mullach an Rathain and a view of the spectacular jumble of hill, rock and water that lies all around. Beinn Alligin in particular looks impressive from this vantage point. Those going on to Spidean a'Choire Leith will find their gaze drawn across the desolate depths of Coire na Caime to this peak and to the jagged outline of the Am Fasarinen pinnacles which lie between Mullach an Rathain and Spidean. The scrambling is not yet over.

Crossing Am Fasarinen is not difficult, although in places the exposure, especially on the northern side, is considerable. To the south numerous paths provide options for avoiding any or all of the scrambling. In wet conditions, however, these narrow paths can be unnervingly slippery.

In all, the pinnacles stretch for nearly 0.8km (½ mile), a delightful scramble up and down rough, reddish sandstone. The holds are generally good, although you need to watch out for the occasional loose rock. The situation is spectacular and the views magnificent, and it ranks as a scramble with the Aonach Eagach, An Teallach and Crib Goch. Once the last pinnacle is crossed, there remains the short climb up the unstable white Cambrian quartzite rubble of the summit cone to Spidean Coire a'Leith and further glorious views.

An easy walk now leads east along the ridge to the start of the path down into Coire Liath Mhor. Those who wish to do so can continue on to the final tops of Bidean Toll a'Mhuic and Stuc a'Choire Dhuibh Bhig, a good viewpoint for Beinn Eighe. It is possible to make a direct descent to the road from this last peak, but it is steep and there is a bit of scrambling. As the route is not obvious from above, I would not recommend descending this way in bad weather. It is also possible to descend to the Allt an Doire Ghairbh from the ridge between the two eastern tops.

Once down in the glen, a 3.5km (2 miles) walk along the road leads back to the campsite. On the day I did this route I felt so exhilarated at the end that I skipped down to the road from the ridge in 20 minutes and was back in camp in another 35! Liathach is that sort of mountain.

SEANA BHRAIGH AND BEINN DEARG

Notoriously remote

W.H. Murray, *Scotland's Mountains*

Start/finish:	The A835 west of Loch Glascarnoch
Summits:	Beinn Dearg 1,084m (3,547ft), Cona'Mheall 980m (3,214ft), Meall nan Ceapraichean 977m (3,205ft), Eididh nan Clach Geala 926m (3,039ft), Seana Bhraigh 927m (3,040ft), Am Faochagach 951m (3,120ft), Beinn Enaiglair 889m (2,915ft), Carn Ban 845m (2,771ft)
Distance:	57km (35 miles)
Navigation:	Very difficult
Terrain:	Moderate
Winter:	Difficult
Map:	OS 1:50,000 Sheet 20: Beinn Dearg

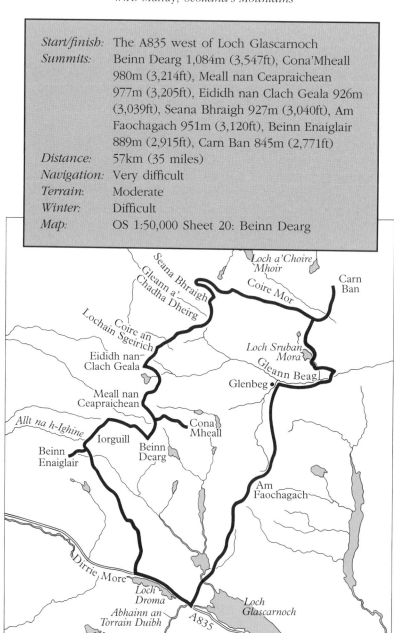

The far north of Scotland is best known for its spectacular coastal scenery and the chain of dramatic mountains that lie just inland from the sea, but these are not all the area has to offer. North of the Dingwall–Ullapool road there lies a wild and remote tangled mass of mountain and loch, the highest point of which is 1084m (3,547ft) Beinn Dearg. Five other Munros, plus three Corbetts, are found in the area, but there are other reasons for venturing into it than peak bagging, as there is much spectacular scenery here and a feeling of remote wilderness and space only found in the empty lands of the north.

Although all the peaks can be climbed on day walks from the road, I feel that this approach misses the best that the area has to offer. Wild camping always gives a deeper appreciation and feeling of contact with an area, but in many places exactly where you can camp is restricted by the nature of the terrain. In the Beinn Dearg area, however, there are innumerable fine potential sites, both high and low level.

On my first visit to this area, the weather was so bad that I ended up staying in the two bothies that lie in the area rather than camping. I did not see much either, as low cloud shrouded the tops. Intentions to return remained no more than that until one July, when I finally resisted the temptation to push on to Ullapool and the magnificent mountains of Coigach and Assynt.

Instead, early one evening I pulled off the road at the western end of Loch Glascarnoch and left the car by the Abhainn an Torrain Duibh. There are many other places a car could be parked. I picked this one as the best for a circular route around the tops with minimal road walking.

The road was left a few kilometres from the car at the west end of Loch Droma, where a path heads up the hillside and along the south-east ridge of Beinn Enaiglair, an 889m (2,915ft) Corbett. Across the Allt Mhucarnaich glen, the steep southern face of Beinn Dearg dominated the view. The path encircles Beinn Enaiglair and where it splits I took the eastern branch, crossing the col between the Corbett and Iorguill, a subsidiary top of Beinn Dearg, before dropping down a short way to camp beside the Allt na h-Ighine.

The grassy site was slightly bumpy, but any discomfort was made up for by the view from the tent of the serrated crest of An Teallach away to the west. The gusty wind rustled the tent at times but ensured that there were no midges – a fair exchange, I felt, although I was not so enamoured of the wind when it grew in strength and the noise of the tent rattling woke me in the night (on reflection, maybe it was the tent I wasn't so pleased with). The sky cleared late in the evening and the temperature in the tent fell to 6°C (43°F) making me glad I had chucked an insulated vest into the pack at the last minute in case it was colder than expected.

Directly above the tent to the south lay the steep slopes and broken crags of Beinn Enaiglair. After breakfast the next morning, I headed directly upwards for the summit by way of a shelving scree and rock rake that split the ragged cliffs. With no pack, and carrying just my camera and a windshirt wrapped round my waist, I was on top in just over 20 minutes. I was glad of the windshirt, as a very cold and strong south-east wind swept over the broad summit. Hazy cloud hid the distant peaks, but Ullapool shone in sunlight and Loch Broom was a startlingly deep blue.

Fully loaded, I headed north-east up the minor top of Iorguill, then east along the edge of the crags above Gleann na Sguaib to the summit of Beinn Dearg, startling a ptarmigan and her tiny fluffy chicks, which ran cheeping in all directions, on the way. Four runners in shorts and T-shirts, and carrying just tiny packs and bumbags, were leaving the top as I arrived. By comparison I felt overdressed and overloaded.

The views from Beinn Dearg are extensive, but as with many rounded hills the scenery close by can only be seen some way from the actual summit. Impressive cliff-rimmed corries lie to the north and east, but you would not know this when on the top. To the north a vast, high tableland stretches 7km (4½ miles) as the crow flies to the remote Munro of Seana Bhraigh. The terrain is complex, however, and time is needed to thread a way round the steep corrie heads, past the many bright lochans and over the summits. Time is needed, too, to absorb fully the wild atmosphere, to take in and become part of this living mountain world.

A steep, stony descent north from Beinn Dearg leads to a flat area where good camps could be made. I lunched here beside a tiny stone-girt lochan, before leaving the pack to climb the scree and grass slopes to the east to the flat summit ridge of Cona Mheall, from where there is a grand view of the huge broken cliffs that make up the east face of Beinn Dearg.

Picking up the pack again, I wandered north-westwards up the gentle slopes of Meall nan Ceapraichean, which by this route feels like a very minor Munro indeed. Not far to the north lies the next summit, Eididh nan Clach Geala, a more distinctive hill. However, the peak that dominates the view north of Beinn Dearg is the soaring spire of Creag an Duine, which, overtopped as it is by nearby Seana Bhraigh, was not granted

*The view from
Seana Bhraigh
across Coire Mor to
Creag an Duine.*

separate mountain status by Sir Hugh Munro.

A brightening sky and easing wind – it had been overcast and very breezy most of the day – late in the afternoon encouraged me to seek another high-level camp. About 1km (⅗ mile) north of Eididh nan Clach Geala lies long narrow, lochan-studded Coire an Lochain Sgeirich. Here I found a fine site on dry, flat grass at 700m (2,275ft) just below the head of the corrie.

Late in the evening, as the bright warm light began to cool and fade, I shouldered my tripod and cameras and wandered down the corrie and on

to the steep western slopes of Meall Glac an Ruighe. Lined up on the skyline to the west were the sharp, distinctive outlines of Ben Mor Coigach, Stac Pollaidh, Cul Beag, Cul Mor, Suilven and more.

Above them, the sun was slowly sinking into hazy cloud. A faint orange glow began to spread across the hills, slowly deepening and spreading as the sun set. The light was marvellous, the land and sky darkening in shades of orange. After an hour the colour began to fade from the sky, and one of the finest sunsets I have seen was over. I stood up and shook myself,

Sunset over Ben Mor Coigach, Stac Pollaidh and Cul Beag from Meall Glac an Ruighe.

surprised at how cold I felt. I checked the thermometer – just 2°C (36°F).

The stunning sunset was the precursor to a magnificent day. The overcast early-morning sky soon cleared to bright sunlight, while the continuing south-east wind kept the air clear of haze and the views sharp and distinct. The sky was an intense alpine blue, the few white cumulus clouds a brilliant white.

Rounding the craggy head of Cadha Dearg to the north east of my camp, where I met the only two people I saw all day, I was soon on the summit of Seana Bhraigh and looking west to An Teallach, its distant buttresses and rock walls quite clear. Further north the hills of Coigach and Assynt studded the skyline, while beyond them were the hazy outlines of the last hills before the north coast, Ben Klibreck and, I think, Ben Loyal and Ben Hope. Below my feet the slopes plunged 400m (1,300ft) down to the dark waters of Loch Luchd Choire, beyond which rose the green, moss-covered ribs of Creag an Duine. A ring ouzel, the white crescent on its breast contrasting with the black plumage, darted among the mossy stones near the summit.

A mix of rock slabs, scree, firm turf and peat hags kept the walking varied on the long, gentle descent east from Seana Bhraigh to the head of Coire Mor. Across the shining waters of Loch Coire Mhic Mhathain, the rocks in its shallows glowing golden in the sun, the snow-streaked slopes of Cona Mheall and Beinn Dearg broke the skyline. Herds of deer were everywhere, some oblivious to my passing, others barking with alarm then trotting away.

A complicated tangle of small crags, tiny pools and heather- and grass-covered terraces lies between Loch Sruban Beaga and Coire Mor. I left the pack beside one of the larger lochans and then scrambled up the rakes to the east until I reached the smoother, gentler, grassy slopes leading to Carn Ban, an 845m (2,771ft) Corbett. The hill streams were bright with small flowers and fresh green moss, making splashes of colour against the grey-green subtlety of the hillside. Below, Coire Mor stretched out into the west, with Seana Bhraigh rising steeply above it to the south.

Collecting the pack again, I headed south for Gleann Beag, the only valley to penetrate deeply into these hills. A line of cracked and disintegrating cliffs lies along the north side of the glen, a barrier broken below Loch Sruban Mora, where a good stalker's path leads steeply down to the glen. A bulldozed track runs east here but I turned west into the unspoilt upper glen, heading for Glenbeg bothy. The heat in the glen was tremendous and enervating and I longed for the breezes that had cooled me on the tops.

As I had suspected, evening in the glen brought clouds of midges, so although there are many excellent potential campsites I stayed in the bothy. At 350m (1,137ft) my third and last night of the trip was the lowest in elevation.

The few hours of semi-darkness brought a change in the weather, and I woke to a cloudy sky and a cool west wind. The weather continued to deteriorate as I headed south from Glenbeg up the open, tussocky slopes to the last Munro, Am Faochagach. The summit was shrouded in a damp, clinging mist. I raced the rain down the southern slopes of the hill, arriving at the car just as the first drops fell. Within half an hour I was ensconced in the Aultguish Inn at the far end of Loch Glascarnoch with a pot of coffee, a fresh salad and the memories of a satisfying backpacking trip.

SUILVEN AND CANISP

The mountain kernel, the perfect, the ultimate
distillation. Suilven, The Rock, is all summit.

Jim Crumley, *Among Mountains*

Start/finish:	Start at Lochinver on the coast at the end of the A837, or near Cam Loch on the A835 2km (1¼ miles) west of Ledmore Junction. The route up Suilven branches off the through-track between these points at the north-west end of Loch na Gainimh
Summits:	Suilven: Caisteal Liath 731m (2,400ft) is the highest top, the optional eastern tops are Meall Mheadhonach and Meall Bheag. Canisp is 846m (2,775ft)
Distance:	26km (16 miles) round trip from the A835, 29km (18 miles) round trip from Lochinver
Navigation:	Easy
Terrain:	Moderate
Winter:	Difficult
Map:	OS 1:50,000 Sheet 15: Loch Assynt

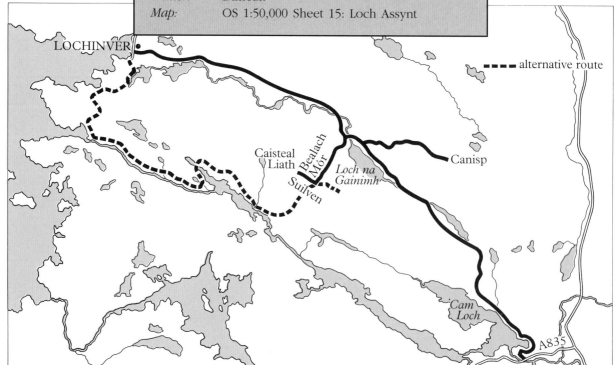

The mist swirled round Cul Mor's summit cairn, cold, damp and thin. A few metres away the grey, stony ground faded into nothingness. There seemed no point in lingering, yet I sensed a change and stayed put, sitting on a chilly rock peering into the whiteness. Gradually the light above grew brighter and stronger, and I began to feel the heat of the sun. Shapes started to form out beyond the rim of the summit, distant castles and towers floating dark and shadowy in the disintegrating clouds. Then, abruptly, the mist had gone, the sun shone harsh and glaring and there, in front of me, were spread some of the strangest and most wonderful mountains in Britain, perhaps in the world, rising isolated and stark out of a flat, wild land of glittering lakes and silvery, twisting rivers: Suilven, dark and dominating, a black, broken-backed slice of a hill floating on a sea of bog and lake; Canisp, a pale wedge of white quartzite and distant Quinag, undulating and shimmering on the horizon; the stickleback ridge of Stac Pollaidh, rising above the wide waters of Loch an Doire

Dhuibh. These are primeval hills, uncompromising hills, bare-boned hills. There is no softness or subtlety about them, and of them all one stands out: Suilven.

Although not even reaching Corbett status at just 732m (2,400 ft), Suilven is the most popular of this strung-out line of hills that lies north of Ullapool in the north-west Highlands. It gives the lie to any idea that height in itself lends grandeur to a mountain. There are few that are as fine as Suilven, be they ten times the height. Such magnificence has its penalties, however, and the easiest way up the mountain is by a wide, eroded scar of a path that leads to the low point of the Bealach Mor. This path branches off the through-route from the A835 to Lochinver, a route that is worth walking in itself, ideally with a side trip up Suilven on the way.

From the north Suilven is a dark, solid mass, a long block of a hill. It is not a subtle mountain: all it has to offer is revealed at once. The ascent is fairly gentle as far as a rocky shelf strewn with lochans below the sudden uplift of

Suilven from the south-west.

163

the mountain. From this shelf the final climb to the bealach, which lies halfway along the mountain, is up a very steep but quite easy stone shoot, decorated in summer with the bright sparkle of yellow saxifrage and alpine lady's mantle, that brings you out suddenly into the wide spaces of the sky as the surprisingly narrow ridge is reached.

On my first visit a strong wind was whipping along the crest and this blew me, exhilarated and exulting, along the narrow and somewhat exposed ridge to Caisteal Liath, the highest point. Looking back, the ridge to the east rose in a straight, steep and amazingly thin line to the sharp spire of Meall Bheag at the far end of the mountain. From the moorland south-east of Suilven this summit rises like a miniature Matterhorn, a startling sight that gives a completely false impression of the nature of the peak as a whole. This top, along with the other one east of the Bealach Mor, Meall Mheadhonach, can be climbed, but the route is exposed

and involves some scrambling. It has to be reversed, too.

The only safe way off Suilven for the walker is via the Bealach Mor. If you are returning to Lochinver, you can descend the southern side of the bealach and pick up a path that leads north-west to the road 4km (2½ miles) south of the village. You could return to Cam Loch and the A835 this way too, but there is no path and the terrain is rough and boggy and the going difficult.

Suilven can easily be linked with Canisp, which lies some 4km (2½ miles) to the east, across the hollow that holds Loch na Gainimh and the path to Lochinver. Although 102m (335ft) higher at 846m (2,775ft), this Corbett is a far less impressive hill, a long whaleback of pale quartzite screes. Why climb it then? For the views, especially of Suilven. It is an easy ascent, a stalking path leading almost to the foot of the north ridge from the north-west end of Loch na Gainimh. If you only have time for one hill, however, it must be Suilven.

North across Loch Veyatie to Suilven.

AN DORUS TO COIRE LAGAN

THE SOUTHERN CUILLIN

Skye is Valhalla, Mecca, the Ultimate

Hamish Brown, *Hamish's Mountain Walk*

Start/finish:	Glen Brittle
Summits:	Sgurr a'Mhadaidh 918m (3,010ft), Sgurr a'Ghreadaidh 973m (3,197ft), Sgurr Thormaid 927m (3,040ft), Sgurr na Banachdich 965m (3,167ft), Sgurr Dearg 978m (3,209ft), Inaccessible Pinnacle 986m (3,234ft)
Distance:	13km (8 miles)
Navigation:	Very difficult
Terrain:	Very difficult
Winter:	Very difficult
Map:	OS 1:25,000 Outdoor Leisure 8: The Cuillin & Torridon Hills

The Cuillin are without question the finest mountains in Britain. Packed into a small corner of the Isle of Skye, they contain every mountain feature imaginable except for permanent snow and ice. The main Cuillin ridge is only 11km (7 miles) long, but in that short distance there are 20 summits, 11 of them Munros. A splendid outlier to the west, Bla Bheinn, brings the Munro total up to a dozen. The ridge is extremely narrow and consists of rock pinnacles and aretes throughout its length. There is nothing on the mainland comparable. The rock scenery is not confined to the ridge, either. To the east, where the Cuillin curve round the great bowl of Coruisk, the rock starts at sea level, while on the west it begins at 365m (1,200ft). The rock itself is mostly gabbro, a rough volcanic rock that gives incredible grip whether wet or dry. You can do things here you would not dream of attempting elsewhere. There are, however, intrusions of basalt in places. This is a much smoother rock, and greasy when wet. Learning the difference between the two is important.

The name Cuillin is almost certainly Norse and is often said to come from 'kjolen', meaning 'keel-shaped'. However, in his excellent study *Scottish Hill and Mountain Names* Peter Drummond argues that it comes from 'kiölen', meaning 'high rocks', which seems very appropriate. 'Skye' also has a Norse derivation, coming from 'Skuy-ö', meaning 'island of cloud', unfortunately also very apt.

For confident and competent scramblers the Cuillin is a superb place. Only one peak requires any rock climbing to reach the top, but many are very exposed and sustained scrambles. The highest peak, 1009m (3,309ft) Sgurr Alasdair, is not on the main ridge but on a spur above Coire Lagan. It is named for Sheriff Alexander Nicholson, who made the first ascent in 1873. For walkers, the least exposed route is by the Great Stone Shoot, the longest scree run in Britain. It is, however, extremely hard work.

Walkers who do not like scrambling could consider the Red Cuillin, big, steep, scree-covered granite hills that can all be walked up. These are situated north and west of the Black Cuillin, as the real Cuillin are sometimes known. There are six Red Cuillin peaks over 610m (2,000ft), the highest being 777m (2,5050ft) Glamaig.

The traverse of the whole ridge, described by W.H. Murray as 'the best day's mountaineering in Scotland', requires rock-climbing skills, as there are several technical ascents and descents involved. Fell runners who are also good climbers have run the ridge and the record is an astonishing 3 hours, 32 minutes and 15 seconds, achieved by Andy Hyslop in August, 1994.

Navigation in the Cuillin can be difficult. The terrain is so complex that even the 1:25,000 scale maps cannot show adequate detail. Most peaks and passes only have one or two ways up for the walker, so finding the right route is important. For that reason, this is the only area where I think a guidebook is as essential as a map. A further reason for this is that compasses are unreliable here due to magnetic rock in places. This does not mean that they are always wrong, of course. Readings should be taken away from the rock and in several places. Even then, treat them with caution until it is clear they are correct. A party with several compasses should take readings with all of them. If nothing else, this may show you just how inaccurate they can be. On arriving once at the Bealach a'Garbh-choire in thick mist I asked my Outward Bound students which way was north.

Everyone checked their compasses then pointed in different directions. 'So which way do we go now?' I asked. They looked blank and a little worried. Eventually they realized that as they knew which way they had come up to the ridge, they knew from the map which way to descend and also which way was north. Those who habitually rely solely on compass bearings in poor visibility, ignoring ground features and the map, will have to adapt their techniques for the Cuillin.

Glen Brittle is a long, partly forested, fairly dull glen running south to Loch Brittle. If the southern end of the Cuillin ridge did not lie just to the east, partly hidden by a foreground of boggy moorland, hardly anyone would ever come here. Because of the Cuillin, though, Glen Brittle is extremely popular. In summer it can be as crowded as Langdale or Glen Coe, despite the minimal amenities. There is a youth hostel and a climbing hut run by the British Mountaineering Council, but no hotel or bar. The only shop is on the campsite which lies on the edge of the sandy beach. This site is often grossly overcrowded, with guylines criss-crossing each other everywhere: far better to carry a tent up into the lonely solitude of the high corries. For once, this might provide better protection from the weather too, as the Glen Brittle campsite gives no shelter from the frequent south-westerly gales that sweep in off the sea. I have seen tents flattened by the wind here and have woken to a half-empty site after a stormy night. A good mountain tent is an asset.

The round of Coire Lagan is often recommended for walkers based in Glen Brittle, but this involves some rock climbing unless some of the peaks are omitted. A better scramble, that allows the walker to stay on the ridge throughout, is that from An Dorus at the head of Coire a'Ghreadaidh over Sgurr a'Ghreadaidh, Sgurr Thormaid and Sgurr na Banachdich to Sgurr Dearg. The scrambling is exciting but not difficult.

The path into Coire a'Ghreadaidh starts at the youth hostel and follows the Allt a'Choire Ghreadaidh past some waterfalls. Once in the corrie, the northerly fork of the stream leads up to the scree slopes below An Dorus, The Door, a deep notch in the ridge. It is possible before turning south to scramble up Sgurr a'Mhadaidh. To follow the ridge beyond the knife-edge of the summit requires rock climbing, however, so walkers should return to An Dorus.

A climber surveys the Inaccessible Pinnacle.

The ridge south of An Dorus is an inspiring roller-coaster of a scramble. I did it once in a storm and found it incredibly exhilarating and exciting. Every so often the clouds would be ripped apart by the wind, to give sudden startling views into bottomless depths. Once Loch Coruisk appeared, shining bright in a rare burst of sunlight.

Sgurr a'Ghreadaidh is sensationally narrow, the sharpest in the Cuillin according to Irvine Butterfield, although the scrambling is straightforward. The hardest section is the initial steep 6m (20ft) climb up the south side of An Dorus. After Sgurr a'Ghreadaidh comes the great tilted slab of Sgurr Thormaid, Norman's Peak, after one of the pioneers of Cuillin climbing Norman Collie, then the splintered and again dramatically narrow crest of Sgurr na Banachdich, which sits halfway along the main ridge.

To the south of Banachdich, the huge north face of Sgurr Dearg dominates the view. A steep scramble leads down to the Bealach Coire na Banachdich, often described as the easiest pass across the main ridge. This may be so, but locating the safe way

View across Coire Lagan to Sgurr Mhic Choinnich and Sgurr Alasdair.

down into Coire na Banachdich from the pass is not simple. In mist it is better to continue on to Sgurr Dearg, just a steep scree slope away.

Sgurr Dearg is famous, notorious some walkers would say, because of the great wedge of rock called the Inaccessible Pinnacle that is the highest point. This is the only Munro where rock climbing is required to reach the top. The 45m (150ft) climb up the East Ridge, first done in 1880, is not difficult (it is graded Moderate, the easiest grade, by rock climbers) but it is very exposed, with huge drops on either side. All but experienced rock climbers will require a rope. One is needed anyway for the abseil off down the West Ridge. Having climbed both (always with a rope), I prefer the 18m (60ft) climb up the West Ridge to the East Ridge. It is steeper and harder (graded Difficult), but much less exposed. Munro baggers will want to climb the Pinnacle. Other walkers may well decide that watching the climbers is more enjoyable.

The last day of the Outward Bound Skye Trek course is usually spent climbing an easy route in the Cuillin, and on one stormy occasion course organizer John Hinde and I took eight students up to the Inaccessible Pinnacle. The weather on the ridge was cold, wet and windy. A damp mist swirled round the base of the Pinnacle and the climb looked singularly uninviting. In the past we had taken groups up the East Ridge. However, this route takes time as it requires a belay part-way up, and John felt that the West Ridge would be quicker. Speed was important, given the storm. 'I'll solo the East Ridge,' he said, 'then throw down the rope and you can climb the West Ridge to show the students where the route goes.'

After a surprisingly long time, John appeared on the summit. The wind, he admitted later, had made the climb a little tricky. I began the ascent. Most of the footholds on the West Ridge are outward-sloping ledges. These were so greasy that I could gain no purchase in my soft, bendy, lightweight boots, hardly designed for this sort of thing, so I had to heave myself up on my arms and in places use my knees. It was a desperate climb. The Scottish Mountaineering Club guide book *Rock and Ice Climbs in Skye* describes it as 'extremely polished and horrific in the wet'. This is an understatement! I must have looked totally incompetent to the students, but my only concern was reaching the top.

Once there, I took over the belaying while John arranged the abseil ropes for the descent. Four students managed the climb while three fell off, one three times before giving up, and were lowered back down. The eighth student sensibly decided just to watch. As soon as a student reached the top, John would tie them on to the abseil ropes and send them back down. Despite wearing a pile jacket, waterproofs, balaclava and gloves I got very cold, and was almost too stiff to move when it was time to descend.

From Sgurr Dearg there are two ways to descend to Glen Brittle. Both are excellent and give superb views across Coire Lagan to Sgurr Mhic Choinnich, Sgurr Alasdair and the great cliff of Sron na Ciche. The first follows the crest of the west shoulder of Beinn Dearg, and then descends down steep, stony slopes to Loch an Fhir-bhallaich on the edge of the moorland above Glen Brittle. The second, and more interesting, descent leads below the Pinnacle and the tottering rocks of An Stac to steep scree slopes that run down into Coire Lagan, a spectacular bowl surrounded by fine peaks. Below the lochan a path leads down to Glen Brittle.

ACKNOWLEDGEMENTS

Many people have shared my hill walks over the years. My thanks to all of them, particularly Chris and Janet Ainsworth, Mark Edgington, Dave, Di and Robin Fuller, Graham Huntington, Andy and Jill Hicks, Alain Kahan, Alex Lawrence, Cameron McNeish, Al Micklethwaite, Roger Smith, Scott Steiner, Denise Thorn, Rowena Thorn, Fran Townsend, John Traynor and Steve Thwaites.

PHOTOGRAPH ACKNOWLEDGEMENTS

All photographs by Chris Townsend except for those on pages 36, 39, 42–3, 44 by Graham Huntington and on pages 51–2 and 54 by Tom Lawton.

FURTHER READING

THIS is a selection of books I have found particularly helpful, informative or entertaining, plus a few of my own that may be of interest.

SKILLS

Ashton, Steve. *The Hillwalker's Handbook*. The Crowood Press, Marlborough, Wiltshire, 1990. *Much useful information, especially on scrambling and snow and ice techniques.*

Barton, Bob and Wright, Blyth. 'A Chance In A Million?' *Scottish Avalanches*. SMT, Edinburgh, 1995. *Essential reading if you go into the Scottish hills in winter.*

Cliff, Peter. *Mountain Navigation*. Peter Cliff, Grantown-on-Spey, 4th edition, 1991. *The best book on navigation.*

Langmuir, Eric. *Mountaincraft and Leadership*. MLTB SSC, Edinburgh, Manchester, 2nd edition 1995. *The official handbook of the Mountain Leader Training Boards of the UK.*

Moran, Martin. *Scotland's Winter Mountains*. David & Charles, Newton Abbot, 1988. *What to expect and how to cope.*

Townsend, Chris. *The Backpacker's Handbook*. Ragged Mountain Press, Camden, Maine, USA, 2nd edition, 1996. *Guide to walking and camping in wild country.*

Townsend, Chris. *A Guide to Hillwalking*. The Crowood Press, Marlborough, 1996. *Advice and information on hillwalking, particularly in the British hills.*

Townsend, Chris. *Wilderness Skiing and Winter Camping*. Ragged Mountain Press, Camden, Maine, USA, 1994. *Comprehensive guide to Nordic mountain skiing and snow camping.*

Walker, Kevin. *Mountain Navigation Techniques*. Constable, London, 1986. *Comprehensive.*

INSPIRATION

Bartlett, Phil. *The Undiscovered Country*. The Ernest Press, Anglesey, 1993. *A thought-provoking look at why we climb hills.*

Brown, Dave and Mitchell, Ian. *Mountain Days and Bothy Nights*. Luath Press, Barr, Ayrshire, 1987.

Brown, Dave and Mitchell, Ian. *A View from the Ridge*. The Ernest Press, Anglesey, 1991. *Stories from the hills.*

Brown, Hamish. *Hamish's Mountain Walk*. Gollancz, London, 1978. *Story of the first continuous round of the Munros.*

Brown, Hamish. *Climbing the Corbetts*. Gollancz, London, 1988. *An entertaining mix of stories and suggestions.*

Crumley, Jim. *Among Mountains*. Mainstream, Edinburgh, 1993. *Philosophical tales from the viewpoint of a non-peak bagger.*

Crumley, Jim. *A High and Lonely Place*. Jonathan Cape, London, 1991. *A personal and poetic defence of the Cairngorms.*

Cudahy, Mike. *Wild Trails to Far Horizons*. Unwin Hyman, London, 1989. *Ultra-distance fell running.*

Dempster, Andrew. *The Munros Phenomenon*. Mainstream, Edinburgh, 1995. *A look at the history of Munro bagging, with some fascinating stories and statistics.*

Drummond, Peter. *Scottish Hill and Mountain Names*. SMT, Edinburgh, 1991. *A fascinating guide.*

Gray, Muriel. *The First Fifty: Munro Bagging without a Beard*. Mainstream, Edinburgh. *Irreverent and entertaining tales.*

Harding, Mike. *Walking the Dales*. Michael Joseph, London, 1986. *Excellent photographs and interesting stories.*

Hewitt, Dave. *Walking the Watershed*. TACit Press, Glasgow, 1994. *Story of the first walk along the watershed of Scotland.*

Moran, Martin. *The Munros in Winter*. David & Charles, Newton Abbot, 1986. *The first winter round.*

Murray, W.H. *Mountaineering in Scotland & Undiscovered Scotland*. Diadem, London, 1979. *Classics.*

Murray, W.H. *Scotland's Mountains*. SMT, Edinburgh, 1987. *Interesting general introduction.*

Stainforth, Gordon. *Eyes to the Hills*. Constable, London, 1991. *Some magnificent photographs and interesting mountain philosophy, especially for the Munroist.*

Stainforth, Gordon. *The Cuillin*. Constable, London, 1994. *Superb photographs and interesting writing.*

Storer, Ralph. *The Joy of Hillwalking*. Luath Press, Barr, Ayrshire, 1994. *A funny and passionate look at the reasons to go hillwalking.*

GUIDEBOOKS

Ashton, Steve. *Scrambling in Snowdonia*. Cicerone Press, Milnthorpe, Cumbria, 1980. *One of the first and best of the many scrambling guides.*

Ashton, Steve. *Hill Walking in Snowdonia*. Cicerone Press, Milnthorpe, Cumbria, 1988. *Comprehensive.*

Bearhop, D.A. *Munro's Tables*. SMC, Edinburgh, revised edition 1990. *The official list, includes Corbetts and Donalds.*

Bennett, Donald (ed). *The Munros*. SMC, Edinburgh, 1985. *Beautifully illustrated guide.*

Bull, S.P. *Black Cuillin Ridge Scramblers' Guide*. SMT, Edinburgh, 1980. *Pocket-sized guide to the one area where a guidebook is really needed.*

Butterfield, Irvine. *The High Mountains of Britain and Ireland*. Diadem, London, 1986. *Sumptuously illustrated guide to all the 915m (3,000ft) peaks.*

Cleare, John. *Fifty Best Hill Walks of Britain*. Webb & Bower/Michael Joseph, Exeter/London, 1988. *Well-illustrated selection.*

Dillon, Paddy. *Walking in the North Pennines*. Cicerone Press, Milnthorpe, Cumbria, 1991. *Detailed and informative.*

Earle, John. *Walking on Dartmoor*. Cicerone Press, Milnthorpe, Cumbria, 1987. *Detailed and informative.*

Evans, R.B. *Scrambles in the Lake District*. Cicerone Press, Milnthorpe, Cumbria, 1982. *A good selection.*

Johnstone, Scott, Brown, Hamish and Bennet, Donald (eds). *The Corbetts and Other Scottish Hills*. SMC, Edinburgh, 1980. *Beautifully illustrated guide.*

Nuttall, John and Anne. *The Mountains of England and Wales* (2 vols). Cicerone Press, Milnthorpe, Cumbria, 1989, 1990. *Covers all the 432 summits over 610m (2,000ft).*

Parker, J. Wilson. *Scrambles in Skye*. Cicerone Press, Milnthorpe, Cumbria, 1983. *Pocket-sized guide.*

Sellers, Gladys. *The Yorkshire Dales: A Walker's Guide to the National Park*. Cicerone Press, Milnthorpe,

Cumbria, 1984. *Comprehensive guide to valley and hill walks, with much interesting background information.*

Turnbull, Ronald. *Across Scotland On Foot: A Guide for Walkers and Hill Runners.* Grey Stone Books, Hoddlesden, 1994. *Entertaining, idiosyncratic guide to four coast-to-coast routes, plus much detail on how to plan your own crossing.*

Wainwright, A. *A Pictorial Guide to the Lakeland Fells* (7 vols). Michael Joseph, London. *Still the best guide.*

Wilson, Ken and Gilbert, Richard (eds). *The Big Walks.* Diadem, London, 1980. *An interesting, well-illustrated selection of 55 long mountain walks.*

USEFUL ADDRESSES

The Backpacker's Club, PO Box 381, Reading, RG4 5YY. *The club for those who want to camp wild. Please enclose an sae.*

British Mountaineering Council, 177–179 Burton Road, West Didsbury, Manchester M20 2BB. *For hillwalkers as well as climbers. Information on courses, insurance etc.*

Glenmore Lodge National Outdoor Training Centre, Aviemore, PH22 1QU. *Courses on all aspects of hillwalking.*

The Long Distance Walkers Association, Membership Secretary, 117 Higher Lane, Rainford, St Helens, Merseyside, WA11 8BQ. *Regular walks from 20 to 100 miles. Please enclose an sae.*

Mountain Bothies Association, Information Office, Ted Butcher, 26 Rycroft Avenue, Deeping St James, Peterborough, PE6 8NT. *Maintains unlocked shelters for the use of hillgoers. Regular work parties.*

Plas Y Brenin National Centre for Mountain Activities, Capel Curig, Betws y Coed Gwynedd, LL24 0ET. *Courses on all aspects of hillwalking.*

The Ramblers' Association, 1–5 Wandsworth Road, London, SW8 2XX. *Campaigns for access and conservation. Local groups with regular meets.*

INDEX

Page numbers in italics refer to illustrations